# DEDICATION

This book is dedicated to the memory of Charles P. DeRochie (1929-1990), sometime president of the short-lived Cornwall Electric Railway Society, and one of the CSR's most dedicated supporters.

A native of Cornwall, and a radiologist by profession, initially on the staff of Cornwall's Hotel Dieu hospital, Charlie became interested in streetcars at an early age, inspired by the small but interesting system which served his home town. One of the co-authors of this book, Anthony Clegg, met Charlie DeRochie in 1945; Omer Lavallée made his acquaintance two years later.

Charlie's dedication to the study of the system, its equipment and operations, won him many friends at all levels of the CSR's management and staff, and, needless to say, gave him ready access to the carbarn and rolling stock, privileges which were shared with his out-of-town friends.

In 1951, Charlie DeRochie moved permanently to Toronto, Ontario, eventually leaving his profession for a second career, this time in hotel security. Charlie was still engaged in this security activity at the time of his early death in 1990, at the age of 59.

Top: Charles P. DeRochie, to whom this book is dedicated, is shown at the controls of CSR No. 25, decorated for the final Cornwall streetcar run on July 27th 1949. (Omer Lavallée collection)

Book designed and typeset in Adobe Garamond Pro, ITC Garamond, and Myriad MM by Eric Clegg, with overall guidance from David Henderson.
Graphic grid designed by Primeau & Barey, Montreal.
Printed and bound in Canada by AGMV Marquis.
Distributed by Lit DistCo.

Copyright © Railfare*DC Books, 2007.

Legal Deposit, *Bibliothèque et Archives nationales du Québec* and the National Library of Canada, 3rd trimester, 2007.

Library and Archives Canada Cataloguing in Publication
Clegg, Anthony, 1920-
Cornwall Electric Railway / Anthony Clegg, Omer Lavallée.
Includes bibliographical references.
ISBN 978-1-897190-26-5 (bound).--ISBN 978-1-897190-25-8 (pbk.)
1. Cornwall Electric Railway--History. 2.Street-railroads-- Ontario-- Cornwall--History. I. Lavallée, Omer, 1925-1992 II. Title.
HE4509.C64C54 2007    388.4'60971375    C2007-901435-6

For our publishing activities, Railfare*DC Books gratefully acknowledges the financial support of the Canada Council for the Arts, of SODEC, and of the Government of Canada through the Book Publishing Industry Development Program (BPIDP).

**Railfare ❋ DC Books**
Ontario office:
1880 Valley Farm Road, Unit TP-27
Pickering, Ontario L1V 6B3

Business office and mailing address:
Box 666, St. Laurent Station
Montreal, Quebec H4L 4V9
railfare@videotron.ca
www.railfare.net

Canada Council    Conseil des Arts
for the Arts      du Canada

Société
de développement
des entreprises
culturelles
Québec

# CONTENTS

5   ACKNOWLEDGEMENTS

7   INTRODUCTION

SECTION 2
9   Cornwall's Background

SECTION 3
11  Cornwall Street Railway Company

SECTION 4
17  Cornwall Electric Street
Railway Company Limited

SECTION 5
23  Cornwall Street Railway
Light & Power Company

SECTION 6
33  The Thirties and Forties

SECTION 7
55  St. Lawrence Park

SECTION 8
57  Cornwall Electric Railway Society

SECTION 9
63  Cornwall Trolleycoaches

SECTION 10
71  Two Decades of Electric Freight

SECTION 11
77  Last Day Ceremony

SECTION 12
84  Roster of Rolling Stock

SECTION 13
93  Bibliography

SECTION 14
94  Authors, Maps and Photo Album

Below: Courtaulds (Canada) Limited is in the background on Montreal Road as CSR No. 31 waits for passengers at the east end of the Second Street line on January 18th 1948. (Anthony Clegg)

Above: CSR No. 32 (StL 1930), one of four cars obtained from Northern Texas Traction in Fort Worth in 1939, is about to load two passengers at the North end of Pitt Street adjacent to the CN Station. Note the car-stop sign at the right – the pole with the white painted band – a common identification for transit stops in Cornwall, Ottawa and Montreal as it was inexpensive to apply, completely bilingual and relatively maintenance-free. (Charles P. DeRochie)

Below: A general view of the CSR's Water Street carbarn, taken on November 18th 1945 from the embankment beside Cornwall Canal. The cars standing outside are, left to right, Nos. Indiana Service Corp. 516 (yet to be relettered CSR No. 37), CSR No. 32 (from North Texas Traction), CSR No. 27 (from Johnstown, New York) and CSR No. 17 (from United Railways of Baltimore, Maryland). (Anthony Clegg)

# ACKNOWLEDGEMENTS

I N preparing this work, the authors acknowledge the impressive resources and scholarship of their Railfare colleague, Raymond F. Corley, whose devotion to the collection of factual minutiae about Canadian railways, especially details about motive power and rolling stock, is unrivalled. Ray's special task in this book was the compilation of the complex roster.

Among our other colleagues, Ronald S. Ritchie critically reviewed and edited the manuscript; James A. Brown edited the photographs; and David R. Henderson gave his unique talents to the layout and design of the volume.

Especially we should mention Ernie Jackson, Vice President and General Manager of Cornwall Electric in the 1980s and his associates Susan Richardson and Della MacDonald for their cooperation in providing items from the Cornwall Electric Archives.

The formatting and page layout of this book was pro-vided by Eric Clegg, while his wife, Sarah, contributed her photographic expertise by improving many of the weaker and weathered images.

The generous cooperation and assistance of many other contributors of information and photographs are noted in the appropriate places, but we'd like to thank them here as well:

Charles P. DeRochie, Allan Toohey, Ernie Modler, Cornwall Electric Archives, William Bailey, Brian P. Schuff, John D. Knowles, Raymond F. Corley, Al Paterson, S.S. Worthen, Railroad Record Club, Steve Maguire, LaMar M. Kelley, Carl Malcolm, Denis Latour, Ted Wickson, C. Robert Craig Memorial Library, R.J. Sandusky and Alan Maitland.

Below: An important element in the CSR's economics was its trolley freight operations, serving many of Cornwall's industries. One of the largest of these was Howard Smith Paper Mills situated in Cornwall's west end adjacent to the New York Central Massena-Ottawa line. CSR locomotives in the photo are Third No. 8 (BWe 1924) and Second No. 9 (builder unknown). (Allan Toohey; Omer Lavallée collection)

Above: Cornwall's first piece of snow-fighting equipment was sweeper No. 1, acquired from an unknown source in 1899. This picture of it doing its duty evidently on Second Street West, was made sometime before 1930, when the unit was scrapped. (Omer Lavallée collection)

Below: Map showing the city of Cornwall in relation to adjacent population centres in Canada and USA.
(Omer Lavallée collection)

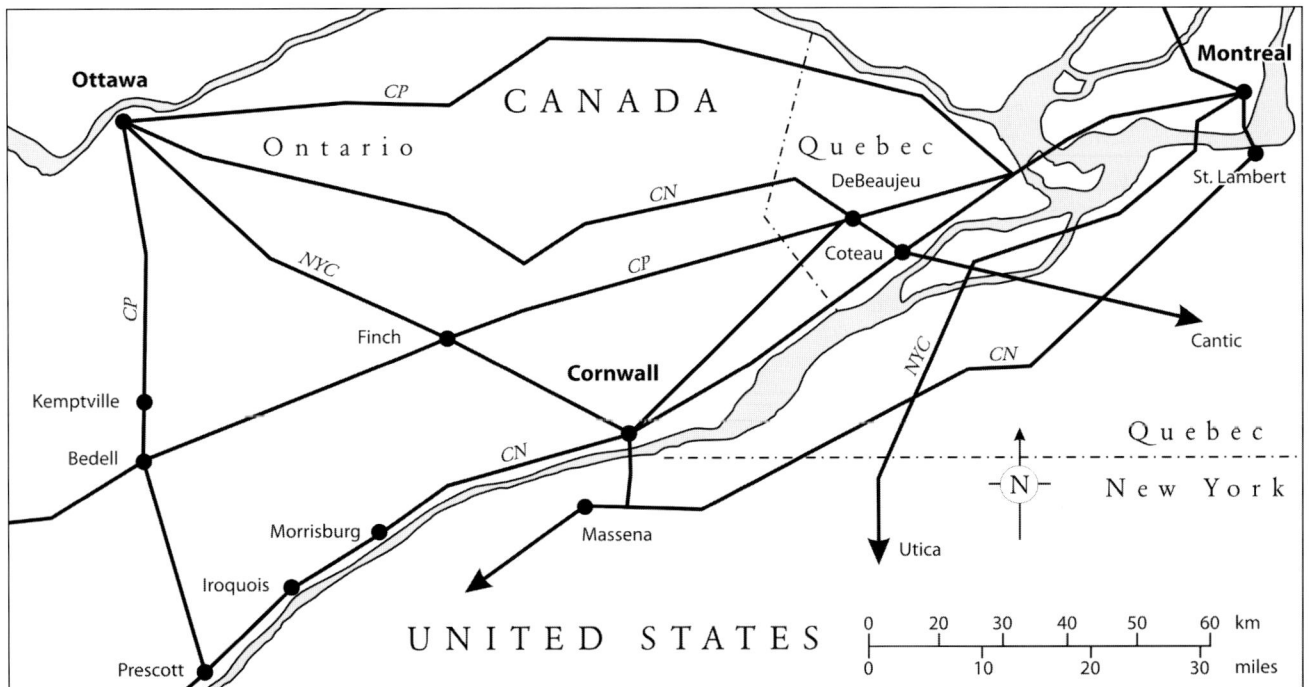

# INTRODUCTION

ONE hundred and ten kilometres (70 miles) south-west of Montreal, on the north bank of the St. Lawrence River, lies the City of Cornwall, Ontario. With a population of approximately 50,000, it is the head-quarters of the St. Lawrence Seaway Authority and one of the principal industrial centres of eastern Ontario.

As far as students of electric railway history are concerned, it was, for three quarters of a century, the scene of operations of a comprehensive electric railway system which, when its locomotives were phased out late in 1971, was the last common-carrier all-electric railway in Canada. For more than fifty years of the line's existence, its services included a passenger street railway whose cars succumbed to trolley coaches in 1949. The trolley coaches served until May 31st 1970 when the company relinquished its franchise and transit operations were taken over by the municipality, using gasoline and diesel buses, as of January 1st 1971.

The authors became acquainted with the Cornwall Street Railway Light & Power Company Limited (CSR) in the 1940s, when it was still engaged in all branches of its rail activities. Its proximity to Montreal, where the authors lived, made visits convenient. The cessation of rail passenger services in 1949, and the preservation — temporarily as it turned out — of passenger car No. 29, stimulated the creation of the Cornwall Electric Railway Society (CERS), in whose foundation and activities the authors were closely involved. Though the CERS existed only briefly, from 1949 to 1952, it claimed to have been Canada's first operating histori-cal electric railway, albeit a parasitical one, as its lone car operated over CSR freight lines, the Society possessing no trackage or real estate of its own.

The moving force in the CERS was the late Charles P. DeRochie of Cornwall, and the preservation of No. 29 and its subsequent occasional operation on excursions was supported and encouraged by the manager and director of the street railway at that time, Charles I. Bacon, and his "second-in-command", superintendent Donald Seymour. Their courage and good grace, at a time when rail hobbyists were looked upon with some suspicion (and, occasionally, not without reason !), is fondly remembered by the authors and their fellow former members of the CERS.

An interesting feature of the CSR's operations is that for virtually all of its existence, it was owned outright by the Sun Life Assurance Company of Canada, an arrangement which resulted in a tranquil and productive existence, not only as a transportation utility but also, as its name implies, as a general electric power enterprise. Efforts by the Ontario Hydro-Electric Power Commission (OHEPC), as early as World War I, to assimilate the CSR and its hydro power

associate, the Stormont Electric Light & Power Company Limited, were successfully resisted.

Sun Life disposed of the transit section of the CSRL&PCo as of December 31st 1970. Cornwall's transit operations were performed by buses operated by A.J. McDonald Limited under contract to the City of Cornwall. The new system is known as Cornwall Transit. On January 1st 1971, the electrified freight switching operations were turned over to Canadian National Railways (CN), which assumed operation on the following April 1st, and diesel power was subsequently substituted for the electric locomotives.

In 1977, Sun Life turned its power distribution facili-ties over to the city and this new organization, known as Cornwall Electric, is still in operation as a power distributor. By the way, Cornwall's original power house of the 1880s had remained in operation until January 1935.

The purpose of this monograph is to give a brief, illus-trated historical review of this small and compact yet interesting rail system.

Anthony Clegg, Omer Lavallée,
Montreal, February 1st 1990.


*It will be noted that seventeen years have passed betweeen the time this manuscript was completed and the publication date, 2007.*

*The text and most of the illustrations were in place in 1990, but the sudden death of Omer Lavallée, on February 5th 1992, caused the manuscript to be put in abeyance for a time.*

*The new partnership between Railfare and DC Books has allowed Railfare to bring the subject back to life, with the addition of a few previously unavailable photographs and up to date items of interest.*

*Anthony Clegg,*
*Montreal, February 1st 2007.*

Above: CSR's Cedars Rapids commercial power plant, with an installed generation capacity of 187 thousand kilowatts. (Cornwall Electric Archives)

Below: This map of the Greater Cornwall area, showing rail lines which served the community since 1855, also indicates the CSR trackage on Second Street, the Belt line and the service on Pitt Street from Water Street to the Canadian National (formerly Grand Trunk) station.

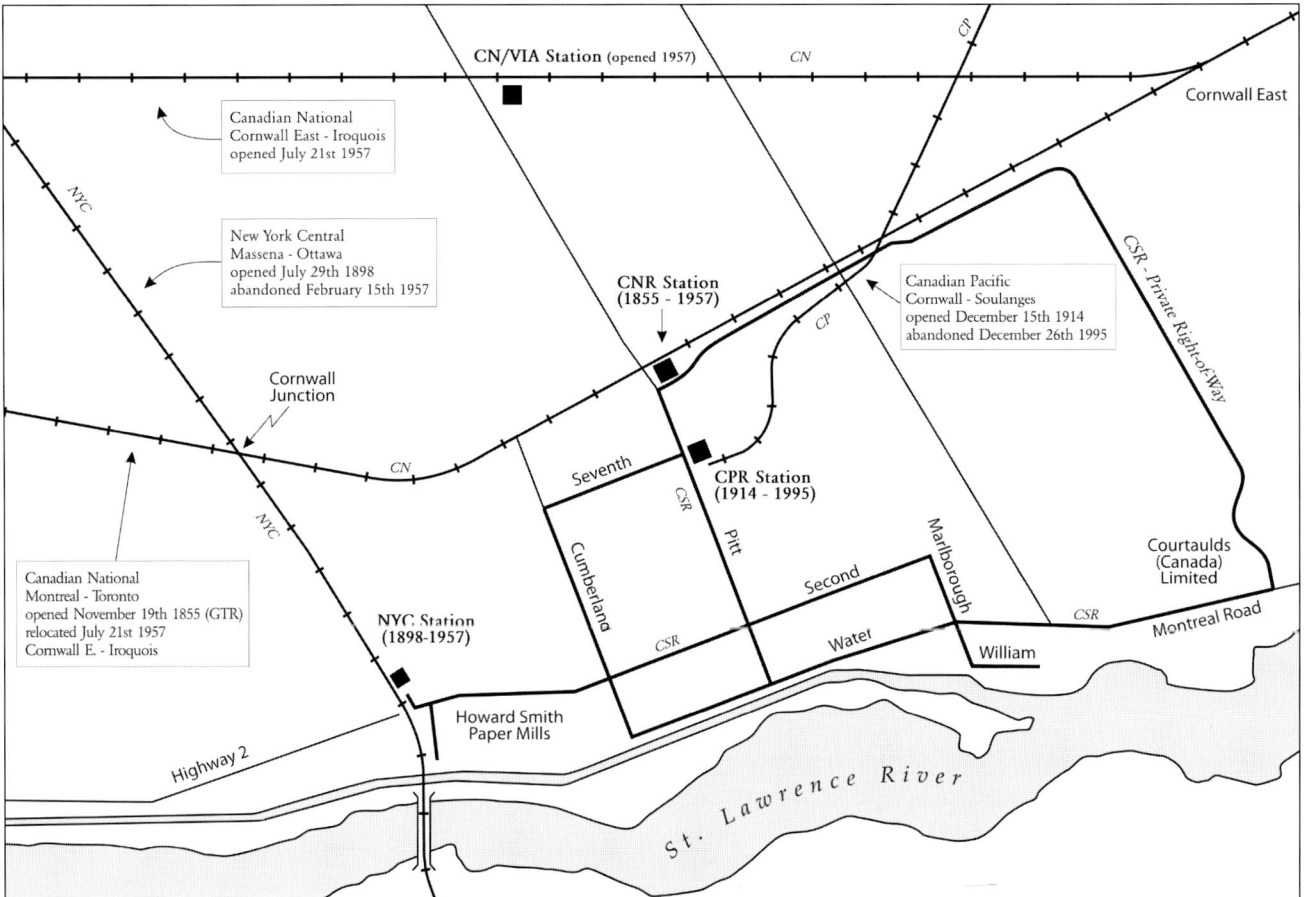

CN/VIA Station (opened 1957)   CN   CP   Cornwall East

Canadian National
Cornwall East - Iroquois
opened July 21st 1957

New York Central
Massena - Ottawa
opened July 29th 1898
abandoned February 15th 1957

NYC

CNR Station
(1855 - 1957)

Canadian Pacific
Cornwall - Soulanges
opened December 15th 1914
abandoned December 26th 1995

CP

CSR - Private Right-of-Way

Cornwall
Junction

CN

Seventh

CSR

CPR Station
(1914 - 1995)

NYC

Cumberland

Pitt

Second

Marlborough

Courtaulds
(Canada)
Limited

Canadian National
Montreal - Toronto
opened November 19th 1855 (GTR)
relocated July 21st 1957
Cornwall E. - Iroquois

NYC Station
(1898-1957)

CSR

Water

CSR

William

CSR

Montreal Road

Howard Smith
Paper Mills

Highway 2

St. Lawrence River

# SECTION TWO

# Cornwall's Background

LIKE many Canadian communities situated along the international boundary, Cornwall came into being originally as a result of the movement of settlers, known as United Empire Loyalists, from the United States into what is now Canada, flowing from the outcome of the American War of Independence. In 1784, the year in which the Treaty of Paris was concluded, thus ending hostilities, the area around Cornwall was surveyed and a one-mile-square (2.59 sq. km) townsite laid out. The community was called New Johnstown after Sir John Johnson (1742-1830), a military commander who had distinguished himself on the British side during the war.[1]

In 1797, the name of the settlement was changed to Cornwall, after Prince George, Duke of Cornwall, the eldest son of King George III.[2] The introduction of steam navigation on the St. Lawrence River in 1809, and its rapid expansion in the ensuing decades, encouraged the building of canals by the public authorities of the provinces of Upper and Lower Canada, to improve the waterway. In 1834, when Cornwall was incorporated as a town, the canal at that place, which allowed river traffic to bypass the Long Sault Rapids, was begun. It was completed in 1843.

Communications with other communities along the river were vastly improved in 1855 when the main line of the Grand Trunk Railway Company of Canada (GTR) was opened between Montreal and Cornwall. Cornwall's total dependence upon the river ceased on October 27th 1856, when the GTR inaugurated through train service between Montreal and Toronto.

The beginnings of major industry came in the 1860s when the first industrial sites were laid out. The manufacture of textiles and of paper, even a century later still among the major industries of the community, began, respectively, in 1870 and 1883.[3] Soon after Thomas Alva Edison had given the first public demonstration of his incandescent lamp invention at Menlo Park, New Jersey, the Canada Cotton mill of Canadian Cottons Limited was the site of a practical installation. This is claimed to have been the first industrial application of electric power. Early in 1884, the installation was completed and officials from Canada and the United States as well as hundreds of Cornwall citizens were present for the initial test. Oil lamps were extinguished, the power turned on and the incandescent lamps emitted their feeble yellow glow.

Firmly convinced of success, Wilbur R. Hitchcock, who had assisted Edison with the installation at the Canada mill, leased the small water-power plant of the Hodge Woollen Mill on the south canal bank and strung power lines along several Cornwall streets. Residents were skeptical, however, and showed little interest in the new form of lighting until 1887 when the Stormont Electric Light and Power Company was incorporated.[4]

The advent of public transit within the community in 1896, by the organization which forms the subject of this book, ushered in a long period of modest but constant industrial expansion. Additional mainline railways came to Cornwall in 1898 and 1914 to compete with the Grand Trunk. The Ottawa & New York Railway Company (O&NY), extending between Massena, New York and Ottawa, Ontario, a subsidiary of the New York Central & Hudson River Railroad Company — later known simply as the New York Central Railroad (NYC) — was opened through Cornwall in 1898.

In 1914, a branch railway was completed linking the community to the Canadian Pacific Railway (CPR) Montreal-Toronto line which bypassed Cornwall some 40 km (25 miles) to the north. This branch, between Cornwall and Soulanges, Quebec, about 1.6 km (1 mile) west of the CN/CP diamond crossing at DeBeaujeu, Quebec, was built by the Sun Life company under the charter of the Glengarry & Stormont Railway Company and was leased to the CPR for a term of 99 years in 1915.

The major industry in the city's east end, the rayon mill of Courtaulds (Canada) Limited, was constructed in 1923.

In 1945, Cornwall was incorporated as a city and, as a result of activity surrounding the construction of the St. Lawrence Seaway and its associated hydro-electric developments in the 1950s, the city more than doubled its population by 1957. This was accomplished by the annexation of a considerable area of the surrounding territory, including Cornwall Island. By 1981, when the decennial census was taken, the city had a population of 46,000 people. Its recent further expansion has been stimulated by the completion of limited-access Highway 401 between Toronto and Montreal in the 1960s.

Right: One of the original electrical generators installed in the Canada mill more than a century ago. (Cornwall Electric Archives)

Above: The original GTR stone station at Cornwall, which was erected in the late 1850s. This building, photographed March 11th 1942, and the more recently constructed adjacent buildings, served the Grand Trunk and the Canadian National until the CN main line was diverted around the seaway construction in the 1950s. (Anthony Clegg)

Below: The New York Central station at the west end of Cornwall was a more modest structure than its GTR counterpart. It was across the tracks from the water tank, which supplied water to locomotives on NYC trains. Photographed on April 20th 1947. (Anthony Clegg)

## SECTION THREE

# Cornwall Street Railway Company

THE first attempt to establish a public transportation system in Cornwall occurred on November 11th 1885, when the Province of Ontario issued Letters Patent incorporating the Cornwall Street Railway Company to build a horse car line in the town. The company was capitalized at $30,000 and its applicants were listed as Charles D. Haines, Andrew G. Haines and Elmer T. Haines, all of Brooklyn, New York; Charles H. Flack of Fort Edward, New York; and Albert W. Flack of Cornwall.[5]

The project called for a passenger and freight street railway in Cornwall and in the adjoining villages of Lorneville, Beaconsfield and Gladstone, and along the roads leading from 9th Street in the township of Cornwall, north to the Grand Trunk Railway; also west from Cumberland Street to the Toronto Paper Company's mill.[6]

In an article dealing with this progressive step in the town's history, the following appeared in the December 14th 1885 issue of an unidentified paper:

"A special meeting was held to-day when a special by-law was passed granting the newly-formed Cornwall Street Railway the necessary permission to commence operations in the Town of Cornwall. The agreement was submitted by the mayor, Mr. James Leitch...." It contained the following points:

1. The railway was to be tax-free for a period of ten years.
2. It was to have the exclusive right to operate in the Town of Cornwall for a period of twenty years.
3. The rules and regulations were to be subject to the approval of the Town Council.
4. The space between the rails was to be paved and kept in repair by the company.

In the winter the company was permitted to run sleighs instead of the wheeled vehicles. They were bound to run cars at least once every hour between 7 am and 7 pm. The fare was not to be more than five cents for each adult passenger, except from 8 pm to 11 pm when a double fare might be charged.

The trackage was to be laid from the Grand Trunk depot to the foot of Pitt Street, east and west on Water Street to the cotton mills, and along Second Street to the paper mill. The company thus had much latitude as to the route to be taken.[7]

The directors of the company met in Cornwall on February 10th 1886 and elected officers as follows:

| | |
|---|---|
| President | Charles D. Haines. |
| Vice-president: | Charles W. Flack |
| Secretary-treasurer: | A.G. Haines |
| Directors: | D. Flack and J.G. Haines. |

Contemporary reports indicated that the president and secretary-treasurer had been engaged in laying out the first route, "which will extend from the GTR station, south on Pitt Street and then west to the Canada Cotton mill." It was expected by the press that construction would begin at once and that it was probable that "the road will be in running order in two or three months."[8]

No immediate action seems to have been taken, as the press reported at the end of April that "Flack Brothers of Cornwall seem to be regularly booming the street railway business in the West. They have already secured the right to construct a road in Brantford, and are figuring to lay another between Berlin and Waterloo,"[9] all Ontario cities.

It is doubtful if their Cornwall project ever got under way, as after diligent search, the authors have been unable to locate any local references in Canada to operation of such a line. However, a street railway system operated by steam motor (dummy) cars is listed and described in the annual Poor's Manual during three consecutive years, 1889 to 1891.

In the former year, the "Cornwall Street Railway" is described as having a "main line - 3 miles; gauge 4'8-1/2"; rail, 20 lbs. Owns 4 cars and 2 motors. C.D. Haines, pres. General Office, Cornwall, Ont." In the following year the listing adds the name of A.G. Haines as secretary and treasurer, while in 1891 the twenty-pound rail is qualified as being 'T' rail.[10] In and after 1892, no further entries appear. Eventually, the charter lapsed.

While these entries, especially since they were revised and amplified annually, suggest an existing operation, it is known that physical information about minor lines in Poor's was sometimes drawn from the contemporary trade press. Thus, the Poor's entries may have been based on nothing more than assumptions based on reports of purchases of rails and rolling stock, coupled with the usual data from a prospectus.

Had the equipment actually been acquired and delivered to Cornwall but without being placed in operation, the ultimate disposition of the "2 motors" referred to may be explained by existing photographs showing two small tramway-type "dummy" locomotives used for switching around the Rathbun Company's mills in Deseronto, a Lake Ontario town, 210 km (130 miles) southwest of Cornwall. They were obtained in the 1890s from an unknown source.[11]

As to the CSR's "4 cars", they may have remained in Cornwall to be inherited and used as trailers for the first electric cars, an assumption suggested by the fact that the road numbers 1 to 4 inclusive in the later electric railway's roster remain unaccounted for.

Above opposite: The CSR's carhouse was situated on Water Street just east of Pitt. Here, ex-Fort Wayne No. 37 awaits assignment ca. 1945. (Ernest Modler, Omer Lavallée collection)

Below opposite: CSR No. 25 on Marlborough Street near Second Avenue on February 14th 1942. (Anthony Clegg)

Above: Changing ends and adjusting the trolley poles on CSR 31. On June 24th 1943, the tram was in its dark green and cream livery, and wartime motor traffic was sparse on the western section of Second Street, Cornwall. (Anthony Clegg)

Below: This advertisement, dating from the 1880s, shows the type of steam "dummy" tram locomotive which is referred to in the text. (Poor's Manual, 1889)

# NOISELESS STEAM MOTORS,
## For City and Suburban Railways.

Above opposite: CN Train No. 14, eastbound from Toronto to Montreal, is photographed from the tower at Cornwall Junction, May 1st 1949, as it approached Cornwall headed by CN No. 6402. (Anthony Clegg)

Below opposite: The New York Central's Ottawa-Massena train at Cornwall, on July 15th 1950. (Omer Lavallée)

Above: The signal tower at Cornwall Junction, intersection of CN's Montreal-Toronto main line (foreground) and the New York Central's Massena-Ottawa branch, as it appeared in the winter of 1950-51. (Omer Lavallée)

Below: Another view of Cornwall Junction and the CN signal tower from which the upper view on page 14 was photographed. The retired combination car adjacent to the tower was to provide sheltered space for construction equipment. (Allan Toohey, Anthony Clegg collection)

Above: CSR No. 10 was one of the system's original closed cars which provided Cornwall residents with their first taste of electric transit. (Charles P. De Rochie collection.)

Below: CSR First No. 26 (BWe 1899), a box-cab locomotive, is shown in an early twentieth century view pushing snow-laden flat cars after a storm. The Cornwall Street Railway was responsible for maintaining its section of the road, which in winter was often the only portion clear of snow. This picture, taken by Thomas Lafleur on March 1st 1900, tells the story. The locomotive was sold in 1932 to Courtaulds (Canada) Limited. By that time it had been rebuilt with a plain arched roof; side doors and windows had been removed. (Cornwall Electric Archives)

# SECTION FOUR

# Cornwall Electric Street Railway Company Limited

THIS new company was incorporated by Letters Patent of the Province of Ontario on March 25th 1896, and was capitalized at $150,000. The incorporators were listed as Herbert R. Hooper, David A. Starr, Frederick N. Saddall and Adele I. Hooper, all of Montreal, Quebec.

The charter permitted the company not only to construct and operate a street railway, but also to construct street-cars and related equipment. This latter activity was never pursued and the company purchased all its rolling stock from other builders. It also provided for the generation of electricity for heating, lighting and power purposes.[12] The latter provision had been made despite the fact that Letters Patent had already been issued to the Stormont Electric Light & Power Company Limited, on September 23rd 1887, "to construct, maintain, complete and operate works for the purpose of light, heat and power" in the town and township of Cornwall and the county of Stormont.[13] In any event, the Stormont company was brought under the same management as the street railway in 1905 by purchase of control through its shares.

The new electric railway company acted with remarkable expedition. On July 7th 1896, just a little more than three months after the birth of the company, the first electric streetcars were placed in service. Karen Carter-Edwards, in her book *100 Years of Service*, gives the opening date as Dominion Day, July 1st 1896. Probably this was the date of the formal inauguration, when the first car with its new coat of vermilion paint carried Mayor L.A. Ross and other dignitaries on a system tour.[14]

The initial operations were on Pitt Street between Water Street and the GTR station, and on Montreal Road, Marlborough and Second streets between the east end of the town at a site later occupied by St. Lawrence Park (see page 55), and the Toronto Paper Company mill at the west end of town[15]. This was just one of the many industries that the Cornwall Electric would come to serve. Service was provided by seven units of rolling stock (five motor cars and two trailers).[16] The officers of the company included H.R. Hooper, president; D.A. Starr, vice-president and general manager; George Leroux, secretary-treasurer; and Wilbur R. Hitchcock, superintendent.[17] The shops were situated on Water Street just east of Pitt Street, and remained there throughout the independent corporate life of the Cornwall system.

A memento of the early years of the Cornwall system is a timetable dated December 24th 1896. It reminds us of the "good old days" when even a small system such as the Cornwall Electric could boast of a timetable. Items of interest from this souvenir indicate that "The streetcars would run to any part of the Town between the hours of 11 pm and 1 am to suit the passengers." At all times between the hours of 6 am and 10 pm, cars were scheduled to leave the Post Office every fifteen minutes. "Close" connections could also be made at the Post Office for all GTR trains, since cars were scheduled to meet the trains.

Even more evidence that the company tried to serve the public to the limit of its equipment can be taken from the statement that "the morning, noon and night cars will run in connection with the mills as may be convenient to the passengers, and that special cars would also run on certain occasions to suit any large party." A final appeal was made, saying that "a comfortable waiting room was at the office on Second Street, where the public would be welcomed at all times."[18] To entice more passengers onto the little single-truck cars, the directors established a park at the end of the rail line, a practice common in the early electric railway era. A beautiful fifteen-acre site on the St. Lawrence River east of Cornwall was acquired and designated St. Lawrence Park. It was developed during the following years and eventually included a dance pavilion, a merry-go-round, a sporting field and a magnificent beach with a 16 m (54 feet) pier. Some 2,500 people gathered in the park during that first September to witness an international regatta. It was a successful day for the company, both financially and as a public relations gesture.[19]

For a short time, things appeared to run smoothly. Emboldened, no doubt, by the successful launch of operations in Cornwall, the directors of the CESR submitted a proposal to the city council of Peterborough, Ontario, to operate an electric railway between that city and the adjacent communities of Chemung and Lakefield, utilizing existing branches of the Grand Trunk Railway which would be electrified at an estimated cost of $350,000.[20] This project, however, was not to come to fruition.

Operations in Cornwall almost came into confrontation with the law on Sunday, August 14th 1898, when the company operated special cars between the GTR station and St. Lawrence Park for a large party of the Fraternal Order of Foresters who had come from Montreal for the day. The cars employed in this service then continued to be operated all day carrying the general public, a breach of CESR's charter which did not permit Sunday operations.

Above: A single truck closed car around the turn of the century, probably on Second Street. The tram is most likely First No. 16, received from Ottawa Electric in 1898. (Omer Lavallée collection)

Below: A classic design of open tram: fine for sunny excursions to St. Lawrence Park, not so comfortable when cold rains blew off the adjacent St. Lawrence River. (Omer Lavallée collection)

Above: The CSR's first car No. 5 was a single truck open vehicle built by Canadian General Electric in 1896. It was photographed about 1924. It is probable that this car was the same as the unit shown on page 18 (lower) with the added protection provided for the motorman by the closed ends and windows.
(Omer Lavallée collection)

This action raised the ire of members of the Lord's Day Alliance, a strong force in municipal politics in Ontario at the time.[21]

Cornwall town council passed a resolution condemning the action of the street railway but General Manager D.A. Starr refused to give any assurance that the street cars would not be similarly used in the future. This was the first time that the company had refused to act in a conciliatory way towards the council's demands. The incident labelled Starr and the CESR as recalcitrant and would come to haunt them in the troubles which loomed in the future.[22]

During this same period of growth, the town council made arrangements with the New York Central & Hudson River system to have that line cross the St. Lawrence River into Canada just west of Cornwall. Starr, ever on the alert to enhance the electric line's earnings, made plans to extend the CESR to the NYC railway station.[23]

In 1898, the NYC&HRRR opened its rail line extending 97 km (60 miles) between Massena, New York and Ottawa, Ontario. The section in Canada was built under the charter of the Ottawa & New York Railway Company (O&NY).[24] Subsequently, the CSR effected a physical connection with the O&NY at its station at the west end of Second Street, for the interchange of freight cars. Passenger car services were extended to this point, which remained the westernmost extremity on the CSR streetcar routes.

It was at this time that the Sun Life Assurance Company of Canada became deeply involved in the affairs of the street railway and of the Stormont Electric Light & Power Company. The intricate financial transactions between Sun Life and the power and street railway companies are fully recorded in Karen Carter-Edwards' book, *100 Years of Service*, which goes into detail concerning these aspects of the organizations' fortunes.[25]

Suffice it here to record that within two years of the first streetcar operation, the fledgling company was in deep financial straits. In addition to the authorized equity financing of $150,000 in capital stock, the company had issued $100,000 in first mortgage, five percent, twenty-year bonds. All of these bonds had been taken up by the Sun Life Assurance Company of Montreal. In the summer of 1898, the interest being in arrears, the trustees for the bond-holders took possession of the line. W.G. Talbot of the Sun Life company was placed temporarily in charge of operations, replacing Hitchcock.[26] Early in 1899, S.W. Bradley, formerly of the Hull Electric Railway, which operated the line between the nation's capital and Aylmer, Québec, was appointed superintendent of the Cornwall system.[27]

Above: Open car No. 7 as it appeared early in the 1900s after it had been equipped with closed end platforms. The motorman is Joe Martin, while the conductor, with the farebox under his arm, is Hubert Pitts. The boy is unidentified. (Cornwall Electric Archives)

Below: The old carbarn of the CSR on Water Street, Cornwall. The photo was taken on March 17th 1927. (Cornwall Electric Archives)

Above: The CSR's second No. 7 was an electric locomotive built by the Montreal Street Railway in 1898. In 1946, it was sold to Courtaulds (Canada) Limited who in 1960 presented it to the Canadian Railroad Historical Association. It is currently at the Exporail/Canadian Railway Museum at St. Constant, Quebec. Still awaiting restoration after more than thirty years, it is Canada's oldest existing electric locomotive. (William Bailey, Anthony Clegg collection)

Below: The new carhouse of the Cornwall Street Railway on Water Street. The photograph was taken on March 17th 1927, the same date as the old carhouse appearing opposite page, lower, was photographed. (Cornwall Electric Archives)

Though an appeal was launched by the shareholders, who felt that they had been "squeezed out", the courts upheld the takeover[28] and the Cornwall system remained in the hands of the Sun Life Assurance Company for the ensuing seventy-five years. Some property of the original company, which was not covered by the mortgage, was sold by the sheriff. This included the carousel and some boats at St. Lawrence Park.[29]

In 1899, the company secured a contract for the movement of Royal Mail between the railway station and the post office.[30] Concurrent additions to rolling stock included an additional motor passenger car and a snow sweeper. Of more significance was the addition of an electric locomotive, marking the Cornwall Street Railway's move into the field of freight switching and transfer service, an aspect which was to occupy an increasingly-important part of its operations as time went on.

Above: Canadian Pacific's wayfreight, Cornwall bound from Montreal, and hauled by CPR No. 432, crosses the CN's Montreal-Toronto double-track mainline (left) and the CSR's Courtaulds loop line (foreground), late in the 1940s. (Charles P. DeRochie collection)

Below: The rear end of a New York Central Railroad passenger train, approaching the bridge over the St. Lawrence River and the Canal — likely the same train shown on Page 14. (Omer Lavalleé)

Bottom: The Canadian Pacific passenger and freight station in Cornwall was a "dead-end" terminal on the east side of Pitt Street just south of 7th Street. The track in the foreground is the overhead-wired CSR interchange track. (Anthony Clegg)

SECTION FIVE

# Cornwall Street Railway Light & Power Company Limited

THE takeover by the bondholders resulted, on April 18th 1902, in a reorganization of the company, with an authorized capital of $200,000, under the above title. The officers at this time comprised James Tasker, president; A. MacPherson, vice-president; W.G. Talbot, secretary and treasurer; and S.W. Bradley, superintendent.[31] The directors of the CSRL&PCo, from this time forward, were also directors and/or senior officers of the Sun Life Assurance Company.

The first challenge which Sun Life had to face was to make the Cornwall transit system operational. Rolling stock, track and power equipment needed to be upgraded; some had to be replaced completely. The new management group encouraged Cornwall groups to make use of St. Lawrence Park and solicited local industries with the idea of providing electricity to power machinery.

Under these policies, the railway's performance improved. Deficits in operations of $7,000, $2,800 and $300 for the fiscal years ending 30 June 1901, 1902 and 1903 respectively, were turned into black figures beginning in 1904.

In 1905, Sun Life decided to purchase the Stormont Electric Light & Power Company which, as mentioned previously, had been incorporated in 1887 to supply electricity to the town of Cornwall. Later in that year, the managements of the electric company and the street railway were consolidated. S.W. Bradley, who had been superintendent of the street railway, was replaced by William Hodge, formerly a director of Stormont Electric and a highly-respected Cornwall businessman. He had also been on the town council, active on the public school board and on the board of governors of the Cornwall General Hospital. His term of management lasted from 1905 until 1917 and he proved to be such a valuable asset that Sun Life later made him a director and vice-president. In that capacity, he served Cornwall and its street railway system until his death in 1930.[32]

By 1911, the street railway was doing very well, indeed, with an operating ratio in that year of 76. While passenger miles increased modestly, the income from freight traffic more than doubled between 1901 and 1911, reflecting the growing importance of this traffic.[33] In the latter year, operations were being carried on with ten passenger cars, two freight locomotives and one snow sweeper.

An additional source of freight traffic for the railway was opened up with the completion of the Glengarry & Stormont Railway Company in 1914. The first proposal for such a line had been mooted in 1909 when the Canadian Pacific Railway's industrial commissioner, H.P. Timmerman, had approached Sun Life with a proposal for a 23 km (14 miles) connection between Cornwall and the former's Montreal-Toronto main line at Apple Hill, Ontario. As neither company was prepared to invest in such a rail line, the matter was left in abeyance. The idea did not die, however, and the Glengarry & Stormont Railway, incorporated in 1912, was completed in 1914 between Cornwall and the CPR line at Soulanges, Quebec, 45 km (28 miles) to the northeast.

This line, built and owned by the Sun Life company, was leased for operation to Canadian Pacific for 99 years from June 1st 1915. Its Cornwall station was situated at the corner of Pitt and Seventh streets. With the opening of this branch, the CPR obtained a five-year option to purchase the Cornwall Street Railway from Sun Life, but it was never exercised.[35]

In 1917, William Hodge decided to retire as general manager of the twin companies, the Stormont Electric, which provided electricity to the town, and the Cornwall Street Railway company. He then became vice-president of the two organizations and was succeeded as general manager by Charles U. Peeling, a man of considerable experience and knowledge and well-prepared for the challenges which lay ahead.[36]

The CPR's interest in acquiring local street railways was revived in 1919, and some interesting facts about the volume and extent of CSR services in that year are contained in a report prepared by J.H. Larmonth for CPR vice-president Grant Hall.[37]

In 1919, Cornwall had a population in excess of 7,000. At this time, the CSR no longer possessed a monopoly on the electric power supply business in Cornwall. Near the town, the St. Lawrence Power Company also had a hydro-electric power development, selling electricity to most of the local manufacturers and also to the CSR. Moreover, the Hydro-Electric Power Commission of Ontario was endeavouring to get established in eastern Ontario and had made arrangements to purchase electric power from an existing private development at nearby Cedars, Quebec.[38]

Larmonth commented that passenger service was light and the larger proportion of the CSR's earnings was derived from the handling of freight. The CSR received a fee of between $3.00 and $8.00 per car for switching, and had a siding into every major manufacturing plant in the community, except one (see map on page 25).[39]

Above: CSR Second No. 8 was built by the Niagara, St. Catharines & Toronto Railway in 1924 and sold to Cornwall ten years later. Until 1946 it was classified as a locomotive, but in that year was reclassified as a snowplow and renumbered P8. It is shown in the CSR yard on Water Street on August 11th 1943. (Brian P. Schuff collection)

Passenger service was provided on two routes, Pitt Street and Second Street, totalling about 6 km (4 miles) of track. One route extended along Pitt Street from the GTR depot to Water Street, east on Water to Brennans Corners, then down to William Street. The other route operated from St. Lawrence Park on Montreal Road to Marlborough Street, north on Marlborough to Second, thence along Second Street to the western terminus at the paper mill and the NYC station.[40]

Cars ran at about ten-minute intervals connecting with all three railway stations and meeting all scheduled trains. The fare structure was as follows:

| | |
|---|---|
| Cash fare, adults......................... | 05 ¢ |
| Cash fare, children..................... | 03 ¢ |
| Six limited tickets....................... | 25 ¢ |
| Five regular tickets...................... | 25 ¢ |
| 21 regular tickets......................... | 1.00 $ |
| 10 children's tickets.................... | 25 ¢ |

As a matter of fact, the basic five-cent-fare remained in effect throughout the life of rail passenger operations, until 1949.[41]

Track was laid with 56- and 60-pound rail, and was at that time considered to be only in fair condition, requiring surfacing and lining. Trolley wire was suspended from posts about 30 m (100 feet) apart and was about 4.9 m (16 feet) above the track. In 1919, the equipment consisted of ten passenger cars, one motor freight car and two locomotives. The passenger cars were operated on the "pay-as-you-enter" system, with the front door lever, operated by the motorman, also raising or lowering a bottom step. Larmonth stated that some cars had a centre aisle with longitudinal seats, while others had an aisle on one side with wooden cross seats holding four passengers abreast.[42] It is probable that the cars with this unusual seating arrangement were rebuilt open cars, Nos. 42, 43 and 44.

All equipment, including locomotives, was hand-braked. The locomotives had a capacity of three loaded railway cars at a time and "seem to meet requirements". During 1918, the system had handled a total of 3,744 cars of freight inbound and outbound, of which the GTR's share was 47.4%, the CPR's 32.4% and the NYC's 20.2%.[43]

In a letter written in February 1919, general manager Peeling claimed to have introduced the one-man car operation on the CSR referred to by Larmonth.[44] Details of this early application of a system which was later widely implemented are unknown, but it is thought that the cars involved were some or all of the following which had been rebuilt by the CSR in 1916:

Nos. 42-44, single-truck closed cars rebuilt from open cars Nos. 5-7, built in 1896 by the Toronto Railway Co.

Nos. 45-47, single-truck closed cars rebuilt from closed cars Nos. 8-10, built in 1896 by the Toronto Railway Co.

Nos. 32 and 34, single-truck closed cars rebuilt from closed cars Nos. 22 and 24. built by Brill in 1894 for the Montreal Street Railway and acquired by the CSR in 1907.

All eight of these cars were scrapped between 1927 and 1930, after the CSR acquired second-hand Birney Safety cars, which are more generally associated with single-truck one-man operations.

A bitter conflict with the Ontario Hydro-Electric Power Commission as a result of wide public discussion at this time over the respective virtues of private versus government ownership of public utilities and transit properties caused Peeling, a devoted private enterprise advocate, to resign and emigrate to Illinois. In 1920, Walter L. Macfarlane was chosen to assume the position of general manager of Stormont Electric and the street railway, to continue the battle against Ontario Hydro and to maintain Sun Life's Cornwall properties in good condition.[45]

In addition to his formal duties, Macfarlane arranged for significant donations to local charities and hospitals. He also arranged for the company to purchase the home on Victoria Avenue where Wilbur Hitchcock, the founder of both the electric company and the street railway, still lived. The old gentleman had fallen on hard times, but was able to reside in his home until his death on June 4th 1944. At that time, he was aged and lonely; his dreams had never brought him material wealth, but he had enriched his community with his progressive thinking and plans.[46]

An important source of traffic was opened up in 1923 when Courtaulds (Canada) Limited completed its rayon mill on the eastern outskirts of town. The line on Montreal Road was extended eastward at this time from St. Lawrence Park to the new mill. In 1932, with the purchase of a motor-baggage-express car from the CSR (No. 26), Courtaulds began to operate its own intra-plant switching. Later, CSR locomotive No. 7 was acquired for the same purpose.

Opposite: Cornwall Street Railway Birney Safety Car 16, built by J.G. Brill, 1920, ex-Toronto Transportation Commission, at main post office, Pitt Street at Second Street, ca. 1938. (CSRL&P official photo)

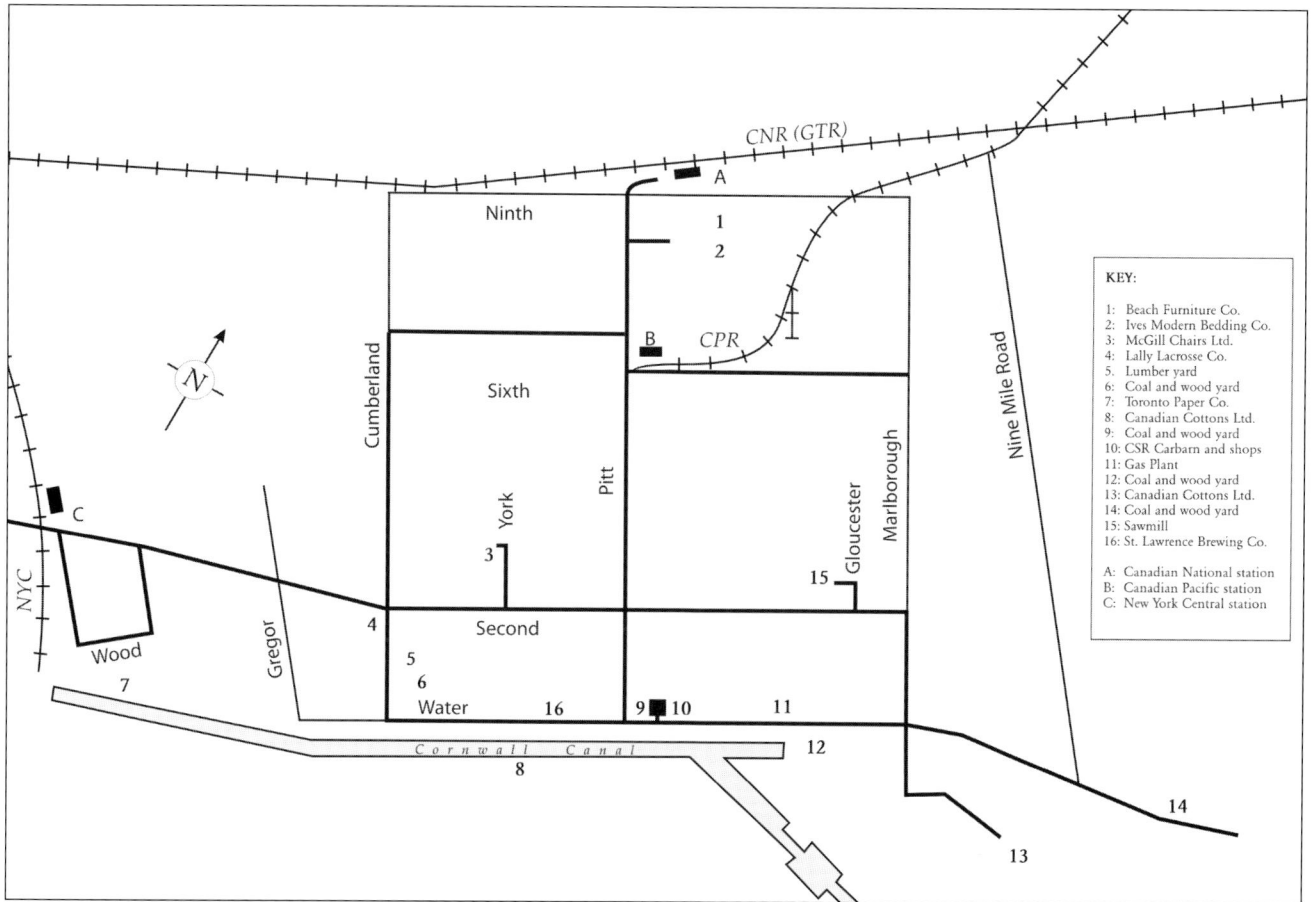

KEY:

1: Beach Furniture Co.
2: Ives Modern Bedding Co.
3: McGill Chairs Ltd.
4: Lally Lacrosse Co.
5: Lumber yard
6: Coal and wood yard
7: Toronto Paper Co.
8: Canadian Cottons Ltd.
9: Coal and wood yard
10: CSR Carbarn and shops
11: Gas Plant
12: Coal and wood yard
13: Canadian Cottons Ltd.
14: Coal and wood yard
15: Sawmill
16: St. Lawrence Brewing Co.

A: Canadian National station
B: Canadian Pacific station
C: New York Central station

Above: Major Cornwall industries, served by the Cornwall Street Railway's freight switching services.

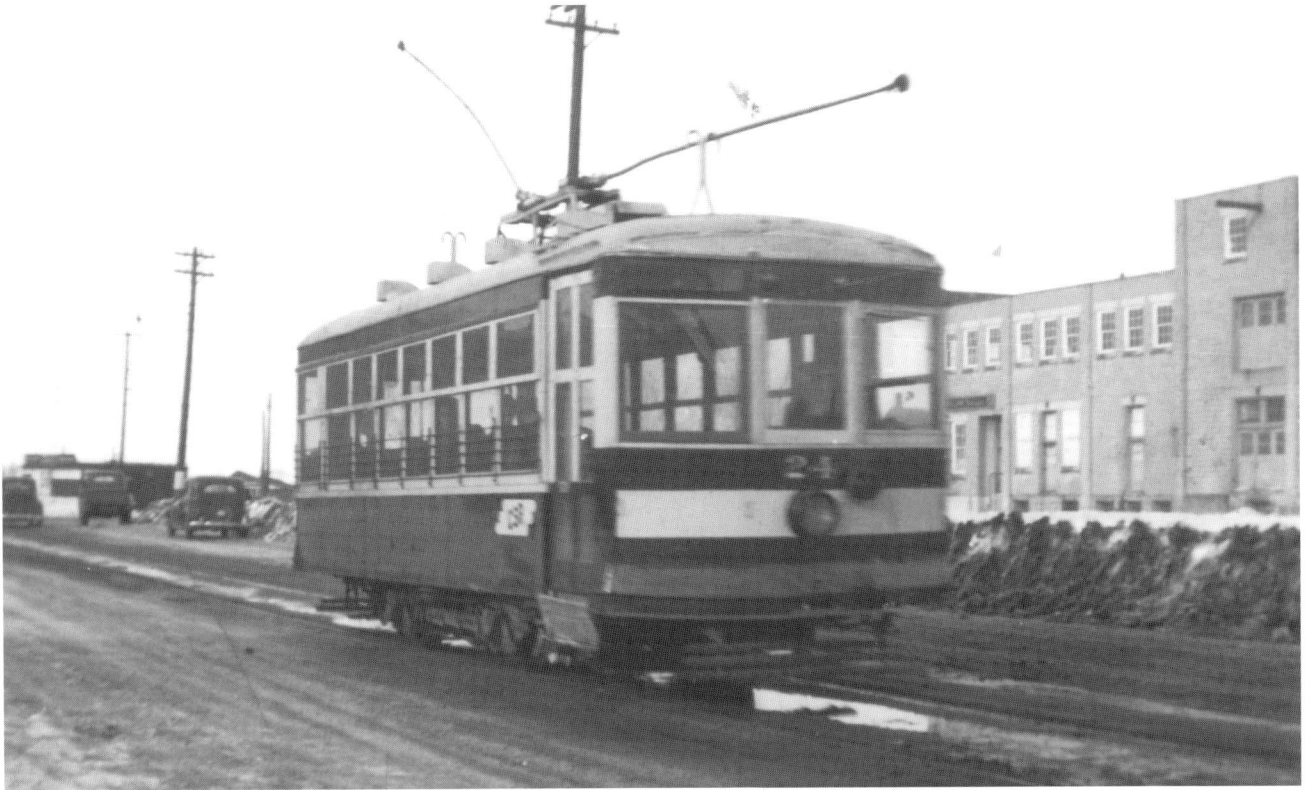

Above: In 1930, Cornwall purchased two Birneys from Green Bay, Wisconsin, and re-numbered them 23 and 24. In 1942, however, CSR 24 still retained the Green Bay No. 37 on the interior bulkhead. It is shown here on Pitt near Eighth Street on February 14th 1942. (Anthony Clegg)

Below: In the mid 1930s, CSR Birney No. 18 (Brill 1920) is eastbound on Water Street at Marlborough. The switch in the right foreground is the Second Street route leading to Marlborough, while the turnout over which the car is passing leads to the cottonmill complex on William Street. (Omer Lavallée)

Above: Courtaulds (Canada) Limited un-numbered unit used for spotting freight cars at the Cornwall east end rayon plant. It had previously been CSR No. 26. Photographed on July 4th 1948. (William Bailey)

Right, centre: Another view of Courtaulds switcher No.26. This was taken on Water Street beside the Cornwall Canal late in the 1940s. Note the rear of the Great Lakes freighter at the left. The photo records one of the rare occasions when the switcher ventured off Courtaulds' property. Judging from the gleaming paint, it may have newly-emerged after repainting in the CSR's shop. (Charles P. DeRochie)

Right, lower: Cornwall's first piece of equipment to bear the number 26, a box-cab electric locomotive built by Baldwin-Westinghouse in 1899, served the system until 1932. In that year, it was sold to Courtaulds (Canada) Ltd. to switch its rayon plant in Cornwall's east end. When built, it had been equipped with a monitor roof and baggage-type doors (See photo on page 16), features it had lost by the time that this photograph was taken in 1948. (Omer Lavallée)

Above: Cornwall Street Railway 17, Birney Safety Car, ex-Baltimore (Maryland) in its red colour scheme, photographed at Water Street carbarn on July 19th 1943. (John D. Knowles)

Left: The CSR operator's daily report of time worked and to list any defects on cars and equipment (approximately 85% of original size).

Below: The CSR weekly pass at 75 cents was a bargain not to be missed. It was good on any car, at any time except on Sundays, and was transferable (approximately 80% of original size).

## Cornwall Street Railway
### CAR OPERATOR'S DAILY REPORT

Name.................................... Date............................. 194

| Car No. | Car No. | Car No. | Car No. |
| From | From | From | From |
| To | To | To | To |
| Time on | Time on | Time on | Time on |

Total     Hrs.     Mins.

### TIME RECORD

| Time at North or West End | | Time at South or East End | | Time at North or West End | | Time at South or East End | | Time at North or West End | | Time at South or East End | |
|---|---|---|---|---|---|---|---|---|---|---|---|
| Hrs | Min | Hrs | Min | Hrs | Min | Hrs | Min | Hrs | Min | Hrs | Min |
| A | M | A | M | P | M | P | M | P | M | P | M |
| | | | | | | | | | | | |
| | | | | | | | | | | | |
| | | | | | | | | | | | |
| | | | | | | | | | | | |
| | | | | | | | | | | | |
| | | | | | | | | | | | |
| | | | | | | | | | | | |
| | | | | | | | | | | | |
| | | | | | | | | | | | |

S.-F.-No. 9538                                    (OVER)

CORNWALL ST. RY. LIGHT & POWER CO. LIMITED
### TRANSFERABLE WEEKLY PASS

From 5 A.M. MONDAY to 12 P.M. SATURDAY
PASS BEARER ON CARS OF THIS COMPANY AT ANY
TIME DURING THE WEEK STATED HEREON
This Pass is to be presented to car operator upon entering
car and is transferable only after the completion
of the trip for which it was presented

PRICE       ANY INTENTIONAL       SERIAL No.
75 cts.     MISUSE OF PASS         4854
            RENDERS IT VOID

## CORNWALL STREET RAILWAY
### LIGHT & POWER CO. LIMITED
## WEEKLY PASS
Good From 5 A.M. Monday To 12 P.M. Saturday

Week - Year

Price       36 - 46   SERIAL
75c                   10584

PLEASE SHOW YOUR PASS

Above: An electric railway requires an adequate voltage for peak periods, but with a minimum amperage loss at all times. Shown here, Alex Mac-Donald inside the Water Street substation, checks to make sure that the ideal conditions are being maintained. (Cornwall Electric Archives)

Below: CSR Birney Safety Car No. 18 (J.G. Brill 1920) formerly operated by the Toronto Transportation Commission, just out of the CSR paint shop in green, cream and blue livery on July 19th 1943. (John D. Knowles)

Above: The interior of CSR's Water Street Carbarn, photographed on July 5th 1947. Rolling stock shown: locomotive No. 9, tram No. 30 and three unidentified Birneys. (Anthony Clegg)

Below: Layout of the CSR carbarn on Water Street, Cornwall, as of the end of June, 1934. Small adjustments to the bulding and trackage were made over the following years. (Cornwall Electric Archives)

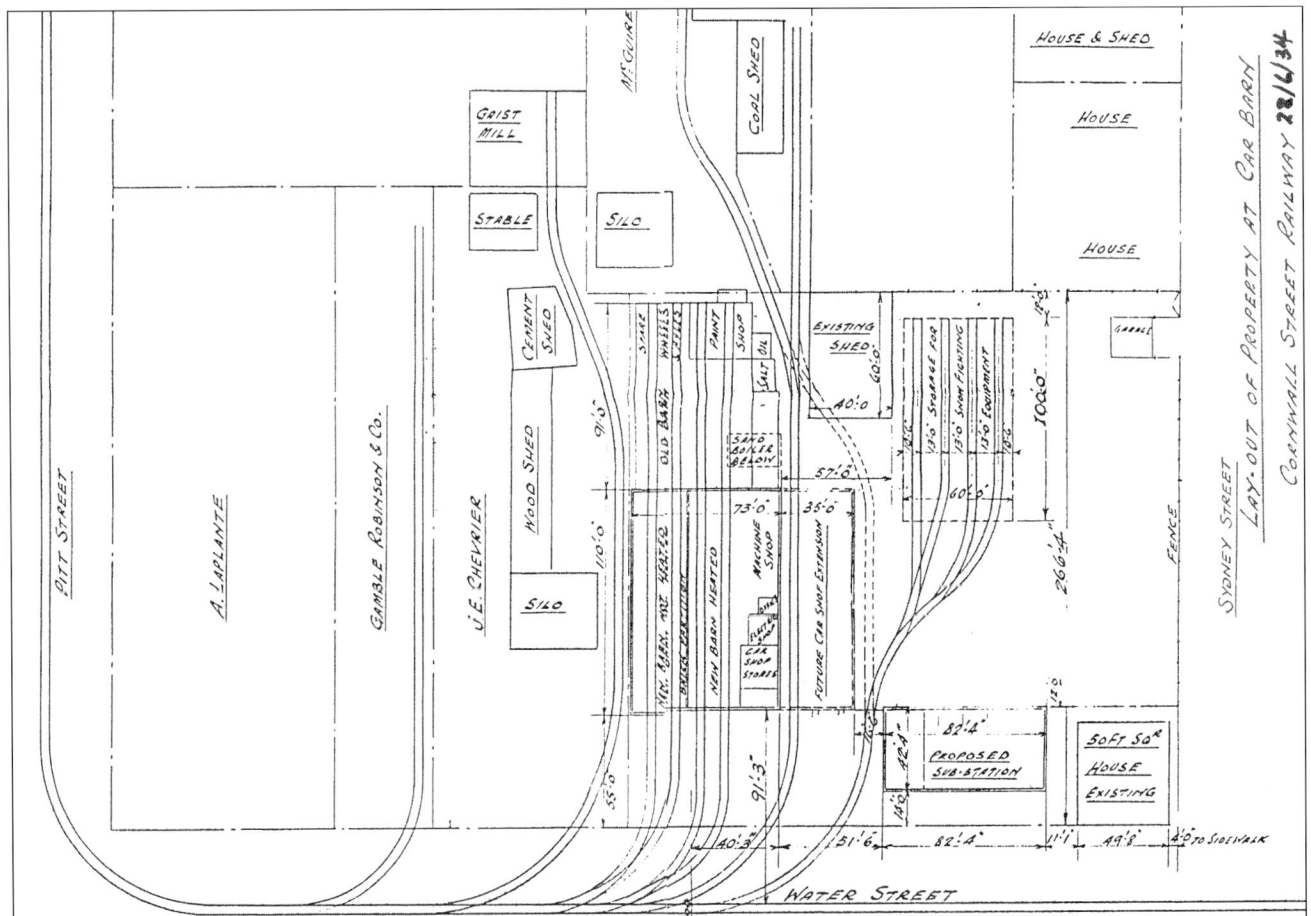

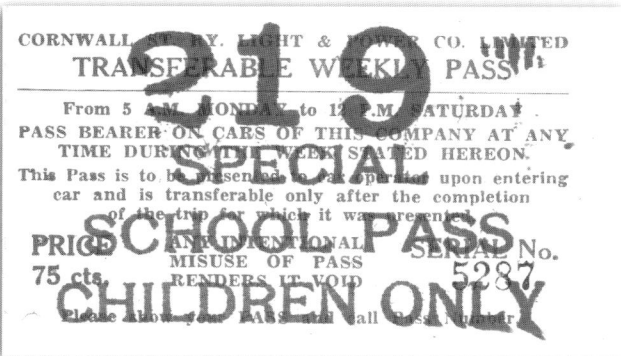

Above: Here, No. 20 (Brill 1920) appears on Second Street in the mid 1930s in what seems to be an adaptation of then-current Toronto livery. It had been acquired from that city (TTC No. 2234) in 1927. (Charles P. DeRochie collection)

Left: Another version of the transferable weekly pass. Cost: 75¢ (85% of original size).

Bottom: The interior view of CSR No. 34 or 35, one of the two trams received from Wilkes-Barre in 1942, photographed at the Cornwall carbarn on May 1st 1949. (Anthony Clegg)

Until 1927, the Second Street line, near its western terminus, operated over private right-of-way on the property of the paper mill near the O&NY station. In that year, the track was placed on Second Street proper and the former line incorporated into the mill trackage.[47] About the same time, the Pitt Street route was shortened to serve only its namesake thoroughfare, though freight switching operations on Water and William streets continued.

The year 1927 was also notable because the Cornwall Street Railway acquired its first steel passenger rolling stock, three single-truck, one-man Birney Safety cars from the Toronto Transportation Commission.[48]

Above: In the 1930s and early 1940s , the CSR's paint shop staff offered some variety in paint designs, using Cornwall's thirteen single-truck Birney Safety cars as subjects. CSR First No. 15 (Brill 1920) is shown southbound on Pitt street at Fifth on March 11th 1942 with a red body, orange window frames, silver roof and silver and black ornamentation. This car had come from New York City in 1928; it was scrapped in 1949. (Anthony Clegg)

Below: CSR No. 38 on Marlborough near First Street East in the dark green and cream paint scheme used when the photograph was taken, on February 14th 1942. (Anthony Clegg)

## SECTION SIX

# The Thirties and Forties

DESPITE the Depression, some services were expanded in 1931 when the number of annual riders, in a town of only a little more than 11,000 people, approached an impressive one million. A "Belt Line" was instituted on the circuit Pitt-Water-Cumberland-Second streets. In 1934, with the extension of track northward on Cumberland to Seventh Street and along Seventh to Pitt, the Belt Line was enlarged to a clockwise circuit on Pitt, Water, Cumberland and Seventh.[49]

With the passing of the Depression and the advent of World War II, the passenger rolling stock was augmented between 1927 and 1945 by additional Birney Safety cars and, finally, twelve second-hand, double-truck cars from systems in the United States and Canada. A glance at the map on pages 44 - 45 and the appended roster will show that Cornwall was, indeed, a "boomer's paradise" as far as its rolling stock was concerned. During its half century of operation, second-hand trolley cars, locomotives and service cars were purchased from more than thirty transit companies in Canada and the United States, possibly a record for such a small-sized system.

Cornwall's first double-truck cars were purchased in 1926 from the transit system in St. Thomas, Ontario. These wooden cars had been built by the Kuhlman Car Company, and were fitted with "maximum traction" trucks. This novel truck design featured one pair of larger wheels and one pair of smaller wheels. As mentioned previously, Birneys from Toronto took over one-man operation in 1927, while other similar single-truck trams were acquired in 1928, 1929 and 1934.

These four-wheeled units became inadequate for the demands of traffic and the acquisition of a light-weight steel double-truck car from Eastern Massachusetts Street Railway in 1937 was followed, in 1938, by three similar cars from Jamestown, New York. Increased traffic caused by the outbreak of hostilities in 1939 saw the CSR purchase four cars from North Texas Traction in Fort Worth, followed in 1942 by two more large cars from Wilkes-Barre, Pennsylvania. In the same year, three single-truck Birneys, surplus to requirements, were sold to Levis (Quebec) Tramways under the directive of the Canadian Wartime Transit Controller. The last trams to be acquired by Cornwall arrived in 1945 from the Indiana Service Corporation in Fort Wayne, Indiana.[50]

In 1941, the ten-year franchise of the CSR was up for extension but the company sought renewal one year earlier, and in spite of some vociferous opposition from a small group of ratepayers, carried the 1940 vote overwhelmingly. One of the CSR officers who played a very significant role in the 1940 franchise campaign was Charles I. Bacon, the assistant manager. Upon the sudden death of W.L. MacFarlane in 1942, Bacon was appointed manager and he directed the fortunes both of Stormont Electric and of the CSR during the following war years.[51]

While company-employee relations were generally good, service was interrupted briefly by two strikes. One, in January 1943, lasted only one day[52], but another in August 1947 lasted three days.[53] During the latter interruption, several industries hired an industrial 0-4-0 saddle-tank steam locomotive to move freight cars to railway interchanges over the tracks of the street railway.

In 1945, Cornwall was incorporated as a city. The population at that time was 15,118 and the CSR system was carrying an impressive 3.3 million passengers annually. They were served by a fleet of twenty-one cars, of which eight were single-truck Birney units.[54] This contrasted with 1.3 million passengers just prior to the war in 1939. The unusually-high proportion of riders to the population could be attributed to the fact that Cornwall industries provided an ample lunch hour, during which period the workers went home. This produced four "rush-hours" per day, thus multiplying the total peak traffic by two.[55] The "nickel fare", mentioned previously, was still in effect, but an even greater transit bargain was CSR's weekly pass, which had been established in 1925. A seventy-five-cent outlay entitled the bearer to unlimited rides from Monday morning until midnight the following Saturday. When Sunday service was inaugurated for the first time in the CSR's history on the first Sunday in May, 1942, the validity of weekly passes was not extended and cash fares only were accepted for travel on the Sabbath.

Accidents are events which no transit system desires, but a risk of operations that few can avoid completely. Fortunately, the mishaps on the CSR were of relatively-minor significance. One incident occurred on a wintry day in 1940. The occupants of a corner house were joined at the dinner table by a boxcar pushed by Cornwall electric locomotive No. 11. Failure of the freight car to keep to the rails on the slippery curve gave the occupants of the dwelling nothing more serious than a big surprise, fortunately.[56]

In 1945, another accident resulted in tram No. 31 being gutted by fire. Again, there were no fatalities but the car was out of service for an extended period of time. It was rebuilt with a revised window design and was returned to service, "as good as new". Having to rebuild and repaint No. 31 caused the CSR to experiment with different paint schemes, both inside and out. The former external livery of olive green with cream and blue trim was discarded in favour of maroon and cream. The interior of the tram, formerly

Above: CSR No. 35, formerly Walkes Barre 350, on the Second Street route, is destined for the Courtaulds plant. (Raymond F. Corley collection)

Below: CSR 25, ex-Eastern Massachusetts Street Ry. No. 6014, is shown in a characteristic pose as it waits for passengers from a train on the adjacent CN Montreal-Toronto mainline. (Allan Toohey, Anthony Clegg collection)

Above: CSR No. 36 on July 22nd 1948. The Kuhlman built unit, with "maximum traction trucks", had come from the St. Thomas (Ontario) Municipal Railway in 1926. (Al Paterson collection)

Below: Interior of CSR No. 25, ex-Eastern Massachusetts Street Ry. Taken about 1937, when it arrived in Cornwall. (Omer Lavallée collection)

finished in natural wood, was painted light grey. The result was favourably received by the travelling public and the new livery was applied to all Cornwall streetcars as they became due for repainting.[57]

The authors recall one incident which happened on the CSR but which didn't involve its equipment. It occurred late in the 1940s. A CPR class D4g 4-6-0 type steam locomotive, pulling a way-freight into the CPR station on Pitt Street, failed to stop. The engine couldn't negotiate the sharply-curved CSR interchange track onto Pitt Street. Instead, it rolled over, coming to rest on its right side against the front porch of a cottage on the west side of the street.

During 1945, much trackage was relaid with heavier 105-lb. T rail, and improvements made in the electrical feeder lines. A total of 19,964 freight cars were handled in the twelve-month period. In 1946, a new freight loop line in the northeastern section of the system provided private right-of-way access to Courtaulds' mill, and avoided the necessity of operating locomotive-hauled trains of freight cars along Second Street. This loop was also provided with a small yard at a new interchange with the CPR.[58]

In spite of these improvements, the post-war period found the Cornwall system rundown and in need of extensive — and expensive — renovation. The streetcar system was in particularly poor shape, and its aging fleet of second-hand cars could not cope with the appeal of the automobile. Passengers looked upon the streetcars as necessary evils: old-

Above: CSR No. 31, which made Fort Worth, Texas its home until 1939, rounds the corner of Marlborough and Second streets, bound for the NYC station, on February 14th 1942. At this time, CSR cars were painted dark green with cream trim with silver letters and roof. (Anthony Clegg)

Below: CSR car 31 on September 3rd 1946, as rebuilt after a 1944 fire, with upper sash deleted. It was also re-equipped with Birney Car seats. This was the first double-truck Cornwall car to be repainted from the green livery to the red colour scheme. (John D. Knowles)

Above: Inexplicably travelling northbound on Cumberland Street on the "Belt Line", on April 17th 1948, while the car's destination sign reads "NYC Station", is CSR No. 34 (Brill 1911).
(Allan Toohey, CRHA collection )

Below: A Great Lakes freighter passes through Cornwall Canal in front of the CSR carbarn on Water Street, in the late 1940s.
(Cornwall Electric Archives)

Above: CSR No. 37 is eastbound on Second Street from the New York Central station in this photograph made about 1949. Note the "Z-frame" boxcars in the background
(Allan Toohey, CRHA collection)

Right: CSR No.30 in front of the Cornwall Hospital at Second and Marlborough streets on May 1st 1949. (Allan Toohey)

Below: CSR Second No. 26, in the then-standard green and cream colour scheme, was photographed on February 14th 1942 on the "Belt Line" at Pitt and Fifth Streets. (Anthony Clegg)

THE THIRTIES AND FORTIES

Above: A Cornwall Electric Railway motorman is engaged in reversing the trolley poles of CSR car No. 33. This is in preparation for the return trip northward on the Pitt Street route, on April 18th 1948. The County Jail, barely in view at the left, gave the name "County Jail Wye" to this intersection at the corner of Pitt and Water streets. (Allan Toohey, CRHA collection)

Above: The Courtaulds mill is at the left as CSR No. 30 (St. Louis 1927) leaves the eastern end of the Second Street route bound for the NYC station, about 1949. (Allan Toohey, Anthony Clegg collection)

Below: With the St. Lawrence River in the background, CSR No. 28 is at the eastern extremity of the Second Street route on Montreal Road opposite the Courtaulds plant on January 4th 1949. (Omer Lavallée)

Above: CSR No. 25 (Brill 1922), specially decorated with stars, planets and moons in a "midnight" theme, made the last passenger trip on July 27th 1949. The car left the carbarn at 4:10 pm on that day and after making two revenue circuits of the CSR's "Belt Line", during which time this photograph was taken, returned to the shop at 5:30 pm. (Raymond F. Corley collection)

Below and Right: Two types of Cornwall Street Railway transfers. Both were issued on Second Street trams for transfer to Pitt Street or Belt Line cars (shown approximately 75% of original size).

fashioned relics which had seen their day. When the war was over and civilian shortages were a thing of the past, many citizens were now acquiring automobiles and hoped to see the last of these "antiquated vehicles", their cumbersome tracks and unsightly overhead wires.[59]

Charles I. Bacon, the manager of the system, also concluded that the ridership appeal of the cars was steadily diminishing. In a small city such as Cornwall, the effect of this was that many passengers chose to walk to their destinations rather than use transit.[60] Since the company was also a producer of electric power, it was decided in 1948 to convert the system to trolleybus operation and fifteen Canadian Car & Foundry (CC&F) trolleybuses were ordered in that year with the intention of replacing the streetcar system completely. The coaches would be supplemented by three CC&F-Brill motor buses which the CSR had previously purchased for operation on feeder routes to the streetcars.[61]

The initial trolleycoach service was inaugurated on Second Street on June 8th 1949. Mayor A. Horovitz cut a ribbon with a pair of specially-engraved gold scissors and ushered in a new milestone in the history of Cornwall. E.R. Alexander, CSR's vice-president, then drove the first trolleybus across the intersection of Pitt and Second streets.[62]

Only seven weeks later, on July 27th 1949, rail passenger service came to an end with the inauguration of trolleybus service on the Belt Line. The last run was made by car No. 25, specially painted in black with a midnight theme. After a brief ceremony at City Hall, Sun Life and company officials, members of the council and ordinary citizens boarded the car for its final run on the way to the "graveyard". W.J. Mitchell, CSR superintendent of distribution, dressed as Father Time, sat on a throne erected atop the vehicle. In flowing white robes and wearing a long white false beard, he carried a badly-dented scythe to signify the passing of the old and the introduction of the new. Thus, fifty-three years of rail passenger transit operations in Cornwall were brought to an end.[63]

In these days of $1.00-plus fares, it is interesting to recall that at the time of the changeover from trams to trolleycoaches in Cornwall, the traditional five-cent fare was still in effect, forty-seven years after it was first established.[64]

Below: CSR No. 25, with its route sign indicating "Last Round Up" was photographed at the rear of the Water Street carbarn on August 7th 1949, a few days after the last run. It was scrapped soon thereafter. (Allan Toohey, CRHA collection)

Opposite top: The upper view shows CSR Third No. 2, clearing the CSR storage yard beside the Water Street carhouse March, 1949. (S.S. Worthen)

Opposite lower: CSR car 35, formerly of Wilkes Barre, Pennsylvania, pauses on the Second Street route as sweeper No. l (ex Hull Electric Railway) clears snow from the freight track to the paper mill, March 13th 1949. (John D. Knowles)

Above: Cornwall sweeper E10, formerly of Boston, Massachusetts, on a wintery morning at the CSR carhouse. (Omer Lavallée)

Below: CSR No.2, ex Kingston Portsmouth & Cataraqui (Ontario), waiting for the winter storms to begin, July 19th 1943. (John D. Knowles)

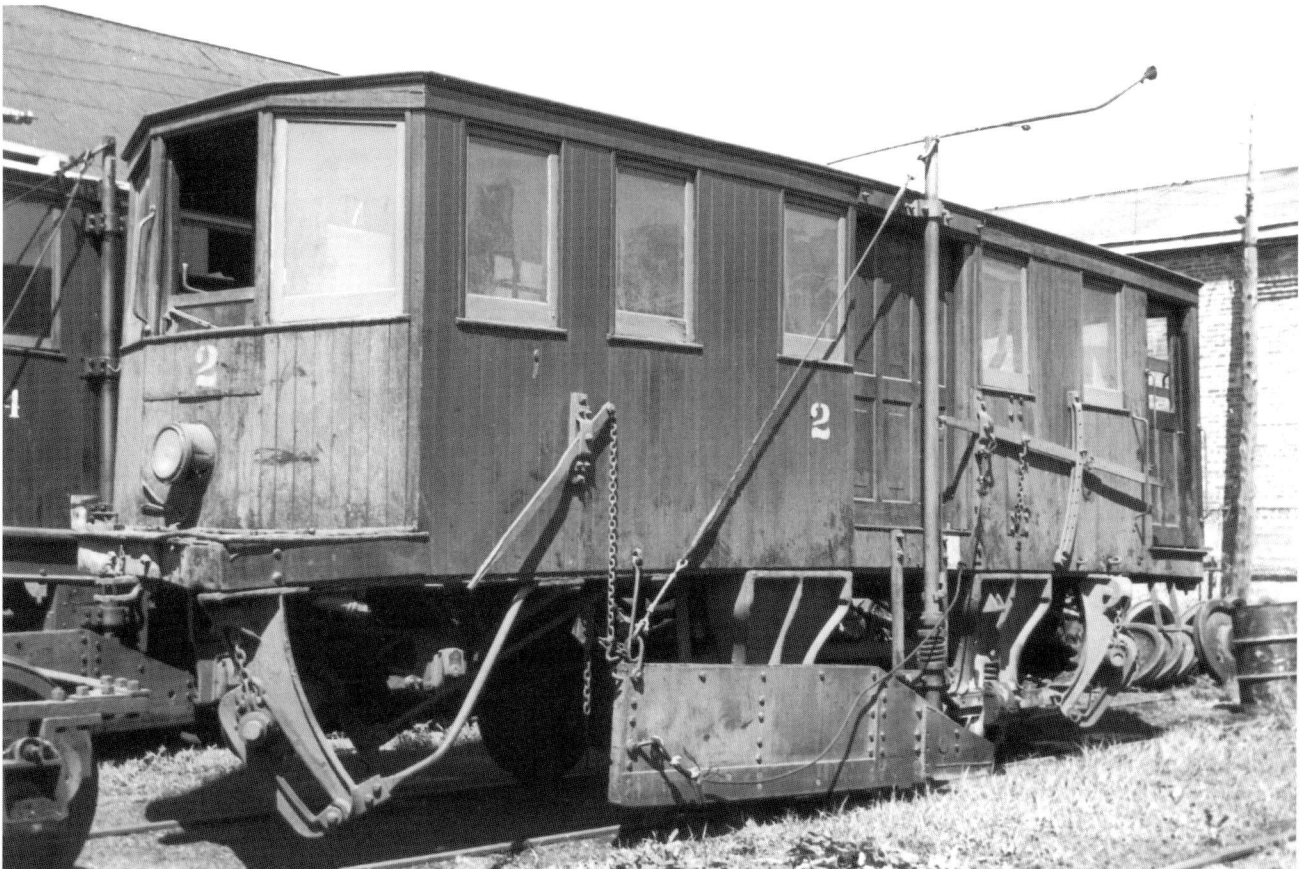

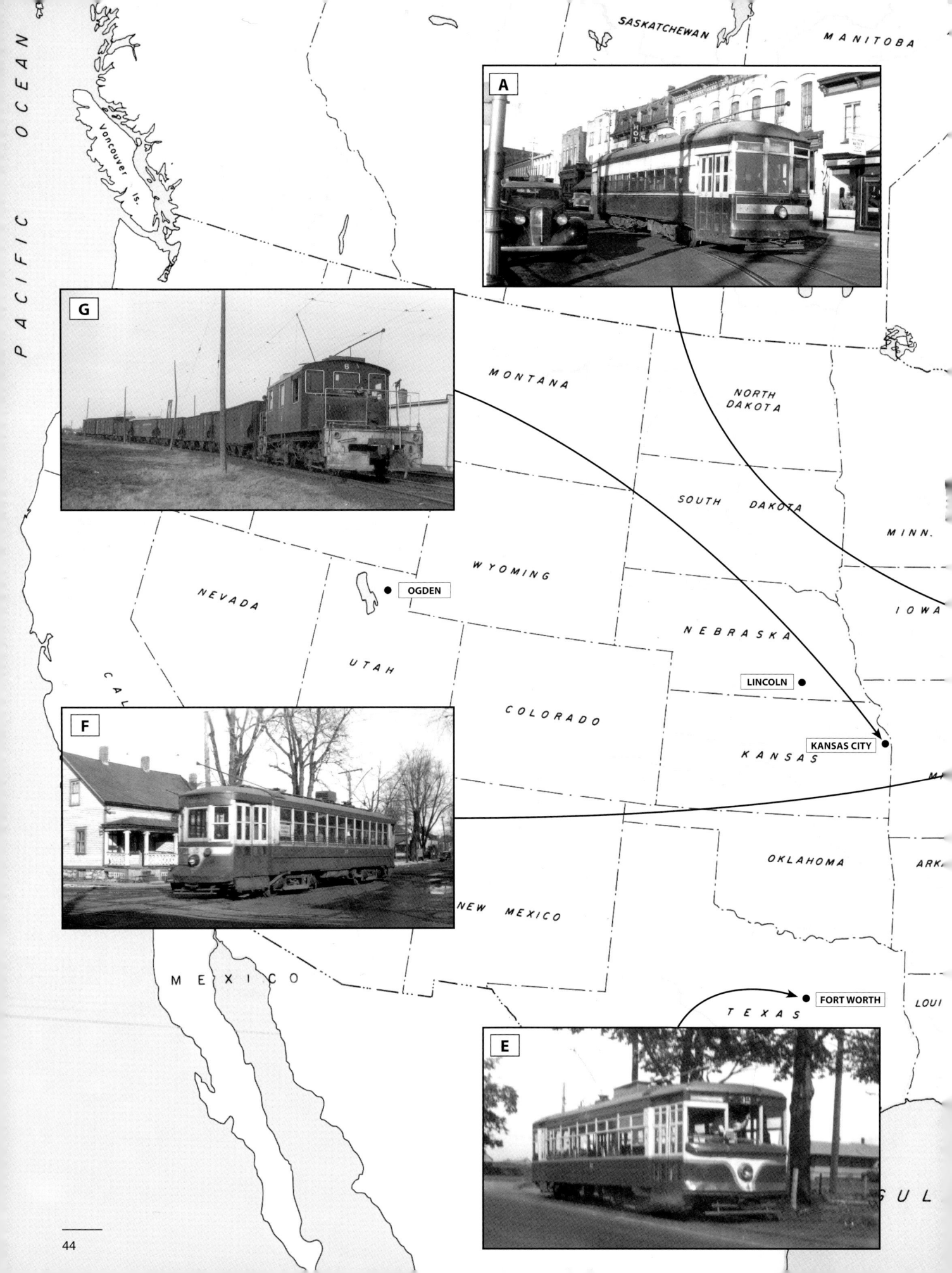

SASKATCHEWAN

MANITOBA

PACIFIC OCEAN

Vancouver Is.

MONTANA

NORTH DAKOTA

SOUTH DAKOTA

MINN.

IOWA

WYOMING

OGDEN

NEVADA

NEBRASKA

UTAH

LINCOLN

COLORADO

KANSAS CITY

KANSAS

M-

OKLAHOMA

ARK.

NEW MEXICO

MEXICO

FORT WORTH

TEXAS

LOUI

GUL

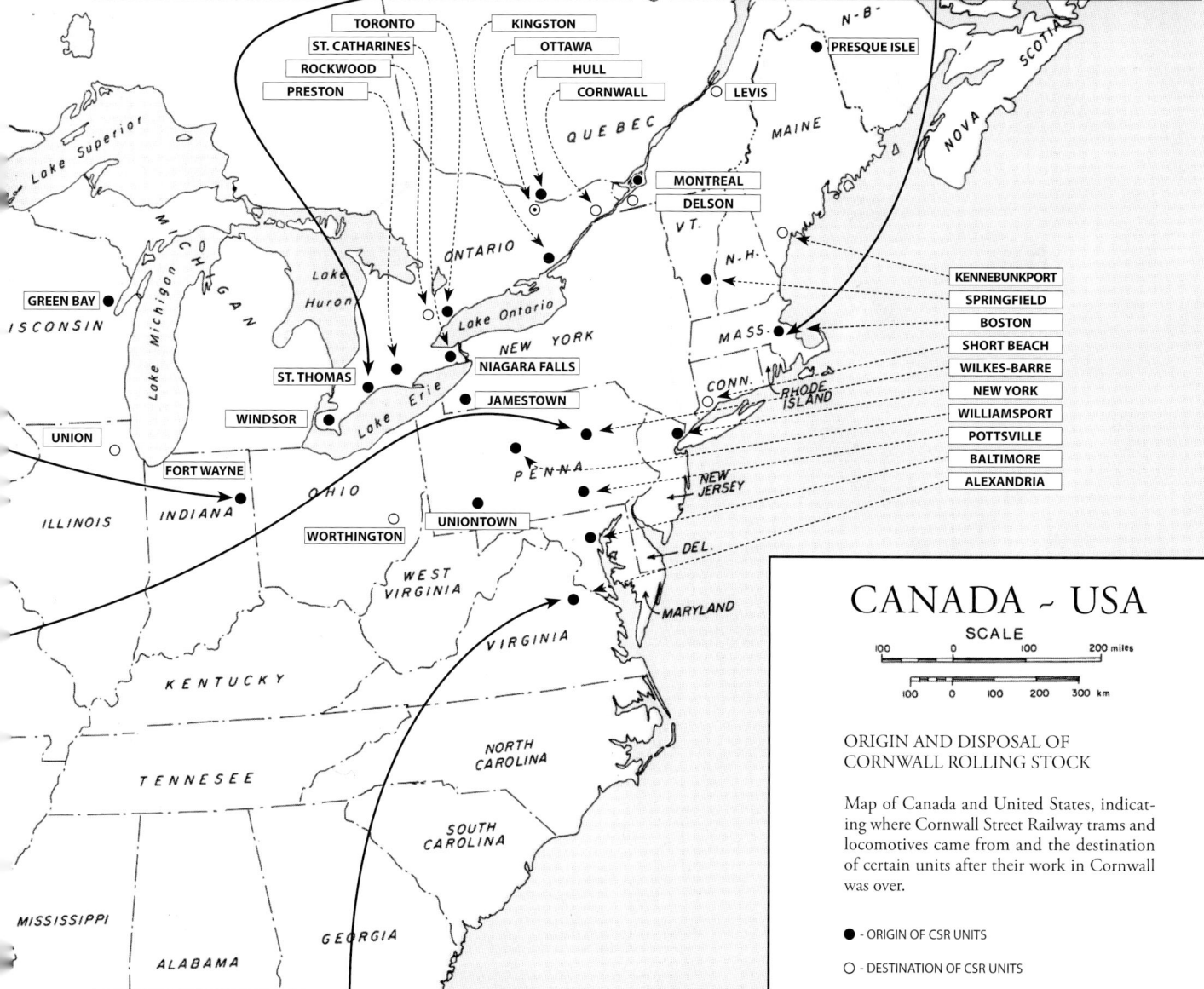

B

C

ONTARIO

TORONTO
ST. CATHARINES
ROCKWOOD
PRESTON

KINGSTON
OTTAWA
HULL
CORNWALL

N - B -

PRESQUE ISLE

LEVIS

QUEBEC

MAINE

NOVA SCOTIA

Lake Superior

MONTREAL
DELSON

VT.

N.H.

MICHIGAN

Lake Huron

ONTARIO

Lake Ontario

NEW YORK

MASS.

KENNEBUNKPORT
SPRINGFIELD
BOSTON
SHORT BEACH
WILKES-BARRE
NEW YORK
WILLIAMSPORT
POTTSVILLE
BALTIMORE
ALEXANDRIA

GREEN BAY

ISCONSIN

Lake Michigan

ST. THOMAS

WINDSOR

NIAGARA FALLS

JAMESTOWN

Lake Erie

CONN.

RHODE ISLAND

UNION

FORT WAYNE

OHIO

PENNA

NEW JERSEY

ILLINOIS

INDIANA

WORTHINGTON

UNIONTOWN

DEL.

WEST VIRGINIA

MARYLAND

KENTUCKY

VIRGINIA

ATLANTIC OCEAN

TENNESSEE

NORTH CAROLINA

SOUTH CAROLINA

MISSISSIPPI

GEORGIA

ALABAMA

D

BAHAMA ISLANDS

# CANADA ~ USA

### SCALE

100    0    100    200 miles

100  0  100  200  300 km

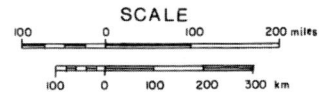

ORIGIN AND DISPOSAL OF
CORNWALL ROLLING STOCK

Map of Canada and United States, indicating where Cornwall Street Railway trams and locomotives came from and the destination of certain units after their work in Cornwall was over.

● - ORIGIN OF CSR UNITS

○ - DESTINATION OF CSR UNITS

| PHOTO | CSR | FROM |
|-------|-----|------|
| A | 33/37 | Ft. Wayne, Indiana |
| B | 36/38 | St. Thomas, Ontario |
| C | E-10 | Boston, Massachusetts |
| D | LOCO 10 | Washington & Old Dominion |
| E | 29/32 | Fort Worth, Texas |
| F | 34/35 | Wilkes-Barre, Pennsylvania |
| G | LOCO 6 | Kansas City, Kansas |

Above: Indiana Service Corp. No. 516 (St.Louis 1923), newly-arrived from Fort Wayne, was photographed at the CSR carbarn on November 18th 1945. This tram and sister ISC car No. 508 were so desparately needed by the Cornwall system that they were pressed into service in their ISC livery and with their ISC numbers. (Anthony Clegg)

Below: CSR tram painters must have had some fun decorating Birney No. 23, received from Green Bay, Wisconsin in 1930. There was a fancy design on the side and an elaborate identity and number patch as shown in this photo taken in July, 1945. (Ernie Modler)

Above: Indiana Service Corporation No. 516 in the process of changing ends on South Wayne Street in Fort Wayne, Indiana about 1940, preparing for the return trip to town on the ISC's route 4 (South Wayne-Broadway). In 1945, No. 516 became Cornwall Street Railway No. 37. (See CSR photo on opposite page.) (Railroad Record Club collection)

Below: The Boston Elevated Railway sold its double truck sweeper E-10 to Cornwall in 1945. This photograph was made in Boston prior to that date. (Charles P. DeRochie collection)

Above: Northern Texas Traction Company car No. 267 is shown in Fort Worth, Texas, in 1938. During the following year, four unidentified cars of this series, perhaps including this one, were sold to Cornwall, becoming CSR Nos. 29 to 32 inclusive. (Steve Maguire collection)

Below: Relatively few units of CSR rolling stock were disposed of in usable condition to other transit properties. One was the CSR's second No. 14 (Brill 1920) which had been purchased from Eastern Pennsylvania Railways at Pottsville in 1934. Only seven years later, in 1941, it became Levis (Quebec) Tramways No. 102 where it was photographed climbing the escarpment on the "Haute Ville" route of the latter system, May 26th 1946. (Anthony Clegg)

**Above:** Standing in the Jamestown (New York) Street Railway's yard in 1933 is JSR car No. 86 (St.Louis 1917). Five years later, it was one of three cars from this system to be sold to the CSR. The others were Nos. 78 and 84. At that time, JSR No. 86 became Cornwall No. 28. All were scrapped in 1949. (Charles DeRochie collection)

**Left:** CSR No. 21 (Brill 1921) had come to the CSR from the Fairchance & Smithfield Traction Company, Uniontown, Pennsylvania, in 1929, where it had been No. 103. Cornwall used it for twelve years, selling it to Levis (Quebec) Tramways in 1941, where it became No. 101. It is shown here in the carbarn at Levis under its last identification shortly before that system was abandoned in 1947, when No. 103/21/101 was scrapped. (Omer Lavallée collection)

**Below:** Indiana Service Corporation No. 508 (St.Louis 1917) is shown at the ISC's carbarn in Fort Wayne, Indiana, on July 29th 1939. In 1945 it was acquired by the CSR and became that company's No. 33. See the same car in CSR service on pages 39 and 46. (LaMar M. Kelley)

Above: Montreal Tramways Company 3152, a Frink Plow, which had been built by the Canadian Car & Foundry in 1925, was sold to Cornwall in 1957. When the Cornwall Street Railway was abandoned, the unit was requested by the National Museum of Science and Technology in August, 1971. The request was cancelled in September of that year, and 3152 was sold to the Branford Railway Museum, Short Beach, Connecticut in 1972. (Omer Lavallée)

Below: CSR 36, one of the pair of Kuhlman-built cars that Cornwall purchased in 1926 from the St. Thomas Street Railway at St. Thomas, Ontario. They were the first double-truck passenger trams in Cornwall and were equipped with "maximum traction trucks" - one pair of large wheels and one pair of smaller wheels on each truck. They served the CSR until 1949. (Al Paterson collection)

**Above:** Ex Ottawa Transportation Commission snow sweeper No. B2 (Ottawa 1926), which continued to carry the same road number while it belonged to the CSR, presented a forlorn appearance in the latter's Water Street yard on September 28th 1970. Two years later, after electric rail service had been abandoned, B2 went to the Seashore Trolley Museum at Kennebunkport, Maine. (Omer Lavallée)

**Below:** The third CSR unit to carry the number 14, this Baldwin-Westinghouse-built locomotive, constructed in 1929, was purchased by the CSR in 1956 from the Springfield Terminal Railway in Vermont where it had been No. 20. Photographed in Cornwall on September 28th 1970, it went to the Illinois Railway Museum in 1972. (Omer Lavallée)

Above: Wilkes-Barre Railways No. 348 (Brill 1911) was a sister of the CSR's Nos. 34 and 35, which had been numbers 344 and 350 in Pennsylvania. No. 348 did not come to Canada, but is shown here in its initial habitat near Nanticoke, Pennsylvania in 1938. (Steve Maguire collection)

Below: Jamestown (New York) Street Railway No. 80 (St.Louis 1917), a sister of the CSR's Nos. 26, 27 and 28, was one of the last cars to run in Jamestown, which, like Cornwall, had a flourishing textile industry. It is shown in the 1930s with the plant of the Cleveland Worsted Mills in the background. (Charles P. DeRochie collection)

Opposite: The hub of the CSR system was the intersection of Second (foreground) and Pitt streets, where all three car routes met in the shadow of the Victorian-era Post Office. This view was taken on May 1st 1949. (Allan Toohey, CRHA collection)

# JUBILEE SHOWS UNITED

## St. Lawrence Park

# All This Week

## 10   Big Shows   10

Merry-Go-Round
Dog, Pony and Monkey
Circus
Over The Top
Wild West
China Town
Splendora
10 in one
Derby Race Track
Monkey Speedway

Fun! Fun! Fun!

Above: A flyer for one of the exhibitions which frequented St. Lawrence Park during the heyday of the popular Cornwall landmark.

Top Right: St. Lawrence Park, established in 1896 by the Cornwall Electric Street Railway, was the site for many Cornwall activities over the years.

Centre Right: This view shows the site photographed from the air.
(Carl Malcolm)

Right: A site map of St. Lawrence Park as it appeared during the 1930s.
(Cornwall Electric Archives)

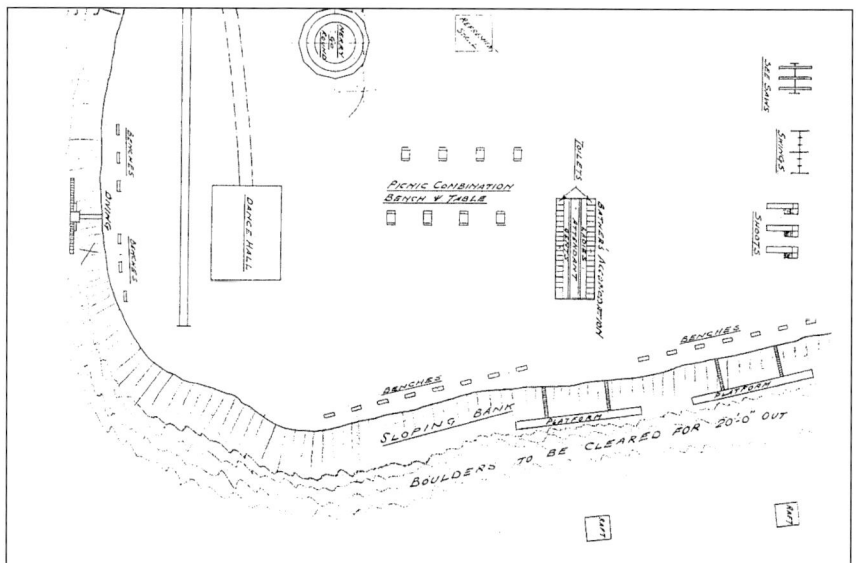

SECTION SEVEN

# St. Lawrence Park

ONE of the features of the Cornwall area during the early years of the twentieth century was St.Lawrence Park, on the plot of land jutting out into the St. Lawrence River between Second Street East and the river itself.

This recreation area had been established by the Cornwall Street Railway in 1896 at the easternmost end of the Second Street car line, and was a tree-covered haven of peace and pleasure for Cornwall residents.

At the time, it was common for transit systems to also own a park adjacent to one of their suburban routes. Ottawa Electric Railway had Britannia Park at the western terminus of the Britannia line, the Montreal Street Railway served Dominion Park on Notre Dame Street East, and the Niagara, St.Catharines and Toronto system had a trolley-car line to Simcoe Park at Niagara-on-the-Lake.

According to the Cornwall Electric publication *100 Years of Service,* the electric railway employed a couple, Mr. and Mrs. Larocque, for the maintenance of the beach and athletic fields which the park encompassed. Not being residents of Cornwall during the hey-day of St.Lawrence Park, the authors of this publication were not able to enjoy the park's facilities, but have been assured by those who visited the area that it was actively appreciated by both Cornwall citizens and visitors alike. Indeed, during the early 1900s, railway excursions to Cornwall and its famed park were common occurrences for the masses.

Facilities of the Park included all the amenities which were expected at such a location. There were slides, swings and a merry-go-round for the youngsters, a parkland with secluded spots and boat rentals for the teenagers, and a dance hall for the grown-ups, who could spend a pleasant weekend evening dancing to the music of the best of local or imported dance bands of the day.

And, of course, there were the beach and change facilities that could be enjoyed by all during the pleasant summer weather. The park's facilities were closed during the winter, but skiing, skating, snowshoeing and other cold weather sports were readily available at the east end of the Second Street car line.

In 1911, Ernest and Lillian Hart took over the maintenance chores, and in 1927 became partners with the Cornwall Street Railway. Karen Carter-Edwards, in her complete history of Cornwall, reports that "over the years the Harts and the CSR kept the Park in good repair and made improvements in the administration of park facilities." Ernest and Lillian continued as custodians and administrators of the area until the end of the 1946 season. After that time, the Cornwall Lions' Club took over and began more

extensive renovations. Time and yearly flood conditions had taken their toll over the years. No longer did out-of-town visitors come by the trainloads to enjoy the park's beauty and recreational facilities, but it was plentifully full of Cornwall residents out for a relaxing day in the sun.

Its restoration, however, was short-lived. In 1957, bathing in the St.Lawrence River had to be prohibited due to the construction of the St.Lawrence Seaway facilities and the resulting flooding and sewage problems.

After much discussion, the Cornwall Street Railway, the Lions Club and the City of Cornwall came to an agreement, by which the municipality took over the park. Further negotiations took place and the City decided that an educational college, allied with a University, would be of greater benefit to the area than a beach and public park.

Therefore, in August 1965, St.Lawrence College purchased the 5 1/2 acres that had been the recreational area. St.Lawrence Park, like the electric tramcars that had served the City of Cornwall, its families and visitors for well over half a century, was gone forever.

Below: CSR No. 9 was the same type as No. 7 shown on page 20. It is pictured at the shelter in St. Lawrence Park about 1900. John Keenan and Jos Martin are the transit employees while Lillian Hart stands in front. The children are not identified. (Cornwall Electric Archives)

Above: CSR 29 on Second Street West on April 17th 1948 (Allan Toohey)

Right: Copy of the instructions regarding the Accident Report, to be filled out by a CSR tram operator in case of a collision with an automobile or in the event of an injury to a CSR passenger (shown approximately 75% of original size).

Below: The motorman's seat and operating controls in CSR 29. Photographed on October 23rd 1949 (Also, see view of the interior of this car on page 92.) (Allan Toohey)

If in accident with an Automobile take note of License No., Name and Address of Owner. Name on driver's permit and address. Number of passengers in automobile. Exact location of accident. Observe carefully the surroundings; note any parked cars nearby or in the block where accident has taken place.

Date of accident, exact time, condition of roads, particularly nearby the accident, weather conditions.

Approximate speed of cars.

Take names and addresses of witnesses.

Take names and addresses of injured.

**Did street car skid?**

**Did the automobile skid?**

**If so, how far?**

**Where were injured taken to and how?**

**Were injuries serious?**

**Where were the autos taken and how?**

## Make No Statements, nor Admissions.

Notify the office as soon as possible.

Notify the police.

All accidents to be reported on this card, either damage to property or injuries to persons.

(over)

## SECTION EIGHT

# Cornwall Electric Railway Society

PROUDLY using the slogan, "Canada's First Operating Trolley Museum", the Cornwall Electric Railway Society (CERS) was founded in 1949, on the eve of the CSR's abandonment of rail passenger operations. The founders included Charlie DeRochie of Cornwall; Arnold Miller and Bill McKeown of Ottawa; George and Edward Thomson; Allan Toohey; Sandy Worthen and the co-authors of this publication, the last-named six people from the Montreal area.

The goals of the CERS included the sponsorship of fantrips over the Cornwall line, and the preservation of a CSR passenger street-car in operating condition. The car chosen for the latter purpose was No.29, built by the St.Louis (Missouri) Car Company in 1930 for the Northern Texas Traction Company (NTT) in Fort Worth, Texas. Car No.29's road number in Texas is unknown, but it was one of four cars of the NTT's 250 series which were purchased by the CSR in 1939. These modern, lightweight, double-ended cars were mounted on roller-bearing trucks and during their service in Cornwall were the mainstay of CSR's Second Street route.

Car No.29 was officially donated to the Society in a ceremony at the Water Street carbarn held in August 1949,

a few weeks after the CSR's official last passenger run on July 27th of that year. The presentation was made by Charles I. Bacon, the CSR's general manager. Participating in the presentation ceremony were E.R. Alexander of Montreal, CSR's vice-president and an officer of the parent Sun Life Assurance Company, and Donald R. Seymour, the CSR's popular and cooperative superintendent.

While the CERS had already held its first fantrip, using car No. 28, on March 13th 1949, subsequent to the abandonment of passenger rail service, No. 29 was the only tramcar available for future excursions, though a few CERS outings utilized electric locomotives. Some of the highlights of these occasions are shown in the accompanying photographs which appear on pages 58 through 61.

Unfortunately, CERS's activities declined in 1951 as a result of two factors: the transfer to Toronto of the group's guiding spirit, Charlie DeRochie, and the initiation of what is now the Canadian Railway Museum's collection. The preservation of an 1892 streetcar in Montreal pre-empted the then-modest volunteer resources. Thus, in 1952, Omer Lavallée, Ronald S. Ritchie and Allan Toohey visited Cornwall and reluctantly returned No.29 to the CSR, writing "finis" to "Canada's First Operating Trolley Museum."

Right: Charles I. Bacon, Vice-President and General Manager of Cornwall Street Railway (1942-1970). Mr. Bacon and his associate, Donald Seymour, were friends of Charlie DeRochie, and were most cooperative with members of the Cornwall Electric Railway Society. (Cornwall Electric Archives)

Below: Rear of one of Cornwall's passes, signed by Charles Bacon.

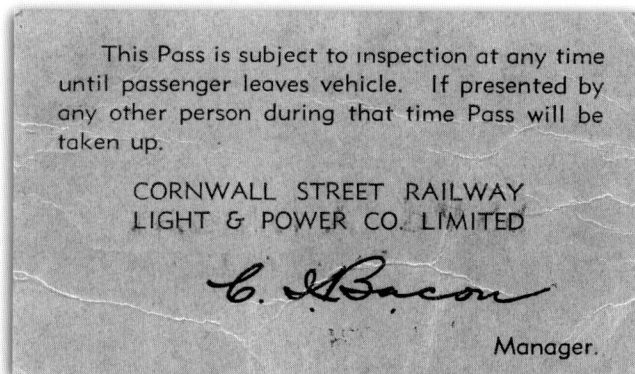

This Pass is subject to inspection at any time until passenger leaves vehicle. If presented by any other person during that time Pass will be taken up.

CORNWALL STREET RAILWAY LIGHT & POWER CO. LIMITED

*C. H. Bacon*

Manager.

Opposite top: The nine founding members of the Cornwall Electric Railway Society just before the association had been formally organized. Eight members are shown on board CSR locomotive No. 11, on January 18th 1949. The ninth, Anthony Clegg, was on the other end of the Kodak. From the left: (upper) Arnold Miller, Bill McKeown, Omer Lavallée, Charles De Rochie, (lower) Sandy Worthen, Allan Toohey, and George and Edward Thomson.
(Anthony Clegg)

Opposite Bottom: Passenger cars were not normally seen at the cotton plant at the end of William Street. It was for this reason that CSR No.28 was taken to this location on March 13th 1949. The occasion was a Cornwall Electric Railway Society fantrip.
(Allan Toohey, CRHA collection)

Above: On September 24th 1950, Cornwall Electric Railway Society car No. 29 crosses Pitt Street beside the CN main line, protected by lowered crossing gates and the gateman's personal attention.
(Allan Toohey, CRHA collection)

Centre Right: Tram No. 29, preceded by Don Ogilvie ringing a little hand bell, travels down a freight-only line in Cornwall.
Photograph taken on September 24th 1950.
(Anthony Clegg)

Lower: A Cornwall Electric Railway Society excursion aboard CSR locomotive No. 9 on February 5th 1950. The Cornwall Street Railway was always extremely co-operative in arranging for many different special moves and most interesting equipment.
(Anthony Clegg)

**Above:** Cornwall Electric Railway Society car No. 29, on the CSR line alongside the Canadian National Railway, crossing the Canadian Pacific Railway in the northeastern section of Cornwall, September 24th 1950.
(Allan Toohey, CRHA collection)

**Left:** CERS No. 29 poses with participants on the Cornwall outing, September 24th 1950. Locale for the group photo was the yard behind the Courtaulds rayon mill. (Anthony Clegg)

**Bottom:** Near the former Canadian National station, Cornwall Street Railway locomotive Second No. 9 on a fantrip on February 5th 1950, pauses to be photographed alongside an eastbound CN Toronto-Montreal freight train headed by General Motors 'A' unit No. 9003.
(Anthony Clegg)

Top: Motor vehicles parked on CSR tracks presented an occasional obstacle to CERS excursions. Here, members are removing a light truck from the path of CERS No. 29 on October 23rd 1949. (Anthony Clegg)

Right: A Cornwall Electric Railway Society work party sprucing up No. 29 on August 14th 1949. Left to right: Omer Lavallée, Charles DeRochie, Allan Toohey, Anthony Clegg in front window, and William "Bill" McKeown. (Anthony Clegg)

Bottom: Another day, another impediment to the progress of CERS No. 29. During the post-1949 freight-only period on the CSR, car owners did not expect rail movements on weekends. Photo taken on September 24th 1950. (Anthony Clegg)

Above, left: The original horse-drawn line wagon, later hauled by a motor truck, shown behind the CSR carbarn on July 19th 1943.
(John D. Knowles)

Above, right: Second No. 5, line car and track grinder, built by the CSR shops in the 1930s.
(John D. Knowles)

Right: CSR Third No. 5 was constructed from car No. 29, after the passenger car was returned to the street railway by the Cornwall Electric Railway Society in 1952. It is shown on May 4th 1967. This unit maintained the electric overhead for the freight-switching locomotives during the latter days of the Cornwall Electric Railway system.
(John D. Knowles)

Below: The CSR's tower car, Second No. 5, built in the Cornwall shops in 1934 on the single truck from one of the original 1896-era closed passenger cars, was photographed late in the 1940s while it was engaged in stringing trolley wire into one of Cornwall's post-war industrial developments.
(Charles P. DeRochie, Anthony Clegg collection)

## SECTION NINE

# Cornwall Trolleycoaches

As outlined in the preceding pages, the 1940s were a hectic time in Cornwall and particularly for the Cornwall Street Railway.

In 1945, the municipality was incorporated as a city, and in 1946 the new freight loop line in the northeastern part of the city eliminated much of the freight movements over the municipal streets. Rail passenger operations were terminated on the Cornwall Street Railway in 1949 but electric trolleycoaches continued to serve the citizens of Cornwall for another two decades. On June 1st 1948 the Cornwall Electric and the Stormont Electric Light & Power Company were amalgamated and the decision was made by the combined management to do away with the tramcars and to establish a trolleycoach system.

An order was placed with Canadian Car & Foundry Co. for fifteen 44 passenger electric buses. These would be supplemented by the three CC&F-Brill gasoline buses which had previously been purchased for use on feeder routes and to augment the streetcars. The first of the new electric vehicles was received early in 1949 and installation of the overhead wires was started soon thereafter. The new vehicles were assigned the numbers 100 to 114 inclusive.

In 1952, an additional trolleycoach was purchased by the CSR to take care of increased passenger volume. This was the sixteenth unit in the Cornwall fleet, and was the Canadian Car's demonstrator coach that had toured Canada during the previous decade to sell the trolleycoach principle to Canadian transit systems.

In Cornwall, this T-44 model coach, built by the Canadian Car & Foundry to Brill design, became CSR No. 115. It was similar to the other CSR vehicles, except that the windows were with sliding sash instead of the vertically-opening windows on the original CSR units. No. 115 was fondly remembered by the drivers for its superior steering ability and quick brake response.

Until 1967, the trolleycoaches served Cornwall well, but by the end of the 1960s, passenger traffic was on the decline and in July 1969, the Cornwall Street Railway informed the Cornwall City Council that it would be unable to renew its transit facilities when the franchise expired at the end of 1970. Effective June 1st 1970, service cuts were put into effect, and the City requested that the trolleycoaches be retired. As it was, the CSR was operating only four of the electric units at that time, and complete cessation of the electric buses took place on Saturday, May 31st 1970. The quiet, dependable units had provided almost 21 years of service. CSR No. 106 was the last trolleycoach in regular service.

Left: As the Canadian Car & Foundry-built electric trolleycoaches were delivered to Cornwall, they were stored outside the CSR's Water Street carbarn, pending vacating of the sheltered space in the building by scrapping the streetcars. This photograph taken May 1st 1949. (Anthony Clegg)

Above: A CSR trolleycoach at the loop at the west-end of the Second Street route. The New York Central station appears at the right-hand side, in this photo taken about 1950. (Cornwall Electic Archives)

Below: This "wire map" shows the CSR's trolleycoach network at its greatest extent, in September 1966.
(Denis Latour)

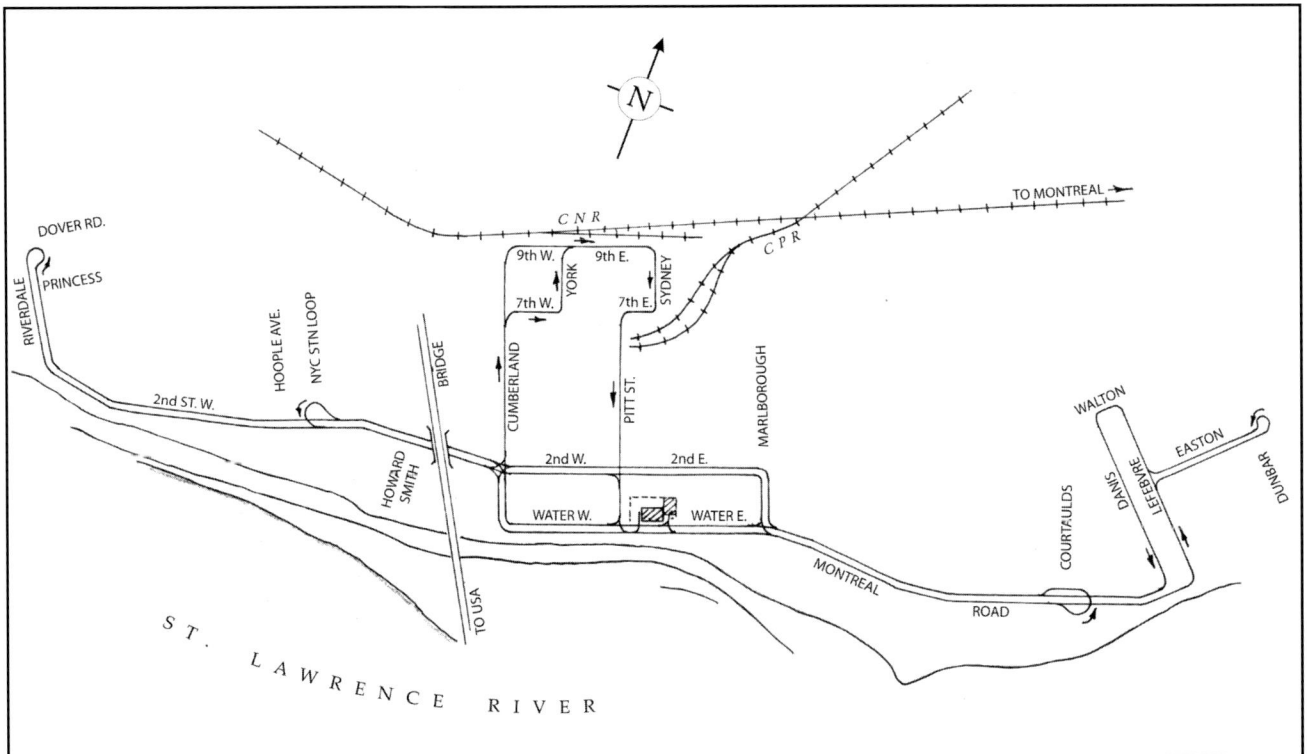

Above: CSR trolleycoach 106 is westbound on Second Street, passing in front of the United Counties Museum building on Saturday, May 30th 1970. This coach was the last one to the carbarn when service was abandoned the next day. In the distance is the highway bridge to New York State. It crosses over the St.Lawrence River and Seaway. (John D. Knowles)

Right: Trolleycoach 102 meets trolleycoach 104 under the elaborate overhead wiring on Water Street. (Ted Wickson)

Below: CSR 104, 108 and 112 at the Toronto Transit Commission's Hillcrest Yard, August 31st 1970. The Cornwall coaches were purchased by the TTC to be salvaged to recover the running gear for use on new Flyer trolleybuses. (John D. Knowles)

Above: Trolleycoaches and gas buses had replaced electric tramcars by the time that this photo was taken in 1950. Compare with the earlier view on page 30. (Cornwall Electric Archives)

Below: Newly-arrived CSR trolleycoach No. 105 (CC&F 1949) stands beside CSR locomotive Third No.12 (BWe 1917) on May 1st 1949. Soon trolleycoaches would replace all streetcars. (Anthony Clegg)

Above: CSR trolleycoach No. 103 crosses the New York Central tracks on Second Street in the 1950s. Note the elaborate protection for the overhead wires. (Cornwall Electric Archives)

Below: Trolleycoach No. 111 loading passengers at the Courtaulds plant on Montreal Road. (Cornwall Electric Archives)

Above: The overhead installation and maintenance crew with their line truck and the trolleycoach overhead wiring, taken in the early 1950s on Water Street, Cornwall.
(Cornwall Electric Archives)

Below: The CC&F demonstrator trolleycoach, which, after a career visiting almost every major Canadian transit system, finally became No. 115 on the Cornwall Street Railway. It was photographed December 15th 1946 at Beaubien and 6th Avenue, Rosemont in Montreal. (Anthony Clegg)

Above: Cornwall trolleycoach No. 100 on Second Street after the trams were replaced by the buses. (Cornwall Electric Archives)

Below: Gasoline bus No. 26 on the North Cornwall route on a snowy, wintery day in the 1950s. (Cornwall Electric Archives)

Above: CSR locomotive First No. 11, builder unknown, was purchased from the Niagara, St.Catharines & Toronto Railway in 1930, and is shown outside the CSR carbarn during the 1930s. No. 11 was scrapped in 1950. (Omer Lavallée collection)

Below: CSR locomotive Second No. 9, crossing Second Street northbound on Cumberland Avenue under the CSR's most elaborate trolley coach overhead wire intersection. The occasion was a fantrip on February 5th 1950. In 1952, this unit was rebuilt into a diesel-electric locomotive by Andrew Merrillees Limited and sent to Bienfait, Saskatchewan (See page 81). (Anthony Clegg)

## SECTION TEN

# Two Decades of Electric Freight

RAIL freight operations, destined to remain for an additional twenty-two years after the cessation of passenger streetcar services, made it necessary to retain a certain amount of street trackage in order to serve all clients and also retain access to the shops on Water Street. However, the passenger abandonments allowed much of the track on Pitt, Second, Marlborough and Montreal Road to be removed. A new line was built along Ninth Street, parallel to the CN tracks, and this permitted abandonment of the line on Seventh. All track on Cumberland and Water streets was retained for freight operations, which in 1949 handled some 24,000 loaded freight cars.[64]

An increase in the industrial establishment in the west end of the city in the 1950s and 1960s necessitated the laying of a considerable amount of additional track in this area. Curiously, much of this development would have been accessible to the line of the New York Central Railroad, but the erstwhile O&NY between Massena and Ottawa had been abandoned on February 14th 1957. Its tracks had been lifted as a result of declining traffic over the whole route, combined with the necessity, imposed by St. Lawrence Seaway construction, to abandon the existing St. Lawrence River bridges and build new, higher structures on a different alignment. Existing rail traffic would not justify those expenditures.

Meanwhile, St. Lawrence Park, Cornwall's riverfront playground at the eastern terminus of the CSR, had fallen on hard times. During the war years, the park became one of the few places which most people could get to. Automobiles had been put away "for the duration", but the reliable trams of the CSR had been available for a ride at the modest price of a "nickel". In 1943, the mayor of Cornwall and the town council asked the street railway to turn the park over to the municipality, a proposal to which Charles Bacon agreed. However, a municipal election, a new mayor and the usual political procrastination finally resulted in the plan falling through; instead, the Park was leased to the Cornwall Lions Club for $1 per annum.

The Lions put a lot of work and money into the rebuilding of St. Lawrence Park, but its restoration to glory was to be short-lived. Construction of the Seaway resulted in the closing of the fine beach which was one of the attractive features of the park. It was no longer a safe place to swim, and water pollution made even restricted bathing hazardous. Once again, the municipality seemed interested in the park, but eventually backed out in favour of St. Lawrence College. In 1965, the CSR announced the sale of St. Lawrence Park to the College for $100,000.[65]

Rail freight operations and trolleycoach passenger services continued to provide Cornwall with local transportation for the better part of another decade. Reflecting the earlier trend with passenger cars, a number of large, second-hand electric locomotives were acquired up to 1962 as well as additional snow-fighting equipment. The most powerful of the locomotives were three seventy-ton units acquired in 1962 from the CPR's Grand River/Lake Erie & Northern operations, which at that time had just been converted to diesel operation. However, by 1970, the same factors which had brought passenger services to an end more than two decades before began to assert themselves as far as freight operations were concerned. The fleet of locomotives was aging and became more expensive to repair. With the decline in electric railway operations throughout the continent, new supplies of good second-hand units were virtually nonexistent.

Increases, too, in the cost of power — now purchased from Ontario Hydro — caused the parent Sun Life company to decide to terminate all Cornwall Street Railway operations, railway as well as trolley coach. Notice was given to city authorities that no renewal of the transit franchise would be sought when it expired at the end of 1970. The last trolley coach, ending CSR transit services, was No. 106 and it made its final run on May 31st 1970, arriving at the shops at 6:02 pm.[67]

No elaborate ceremonies were held to mark the end of trolleybus service in Cornwall, in contrast to the spectacular final runs of the trams and the inauguration of trolleycoaches in 1949. A few employees gathered together to witness the final runs, which were made by drivers Vernon Cooke, Joe Meilleur and Lester Floudes on buses Nos. 100,

Below: Captive to the CSR system was Canada Steamship Lines wooden underframe boxcar No. 5, of unknown origin, photographed at the CSR shops on Water Street on January 18th 1948. (Anthony Clegg)

Above: The CSR possessed eighteen electric locomotives throughout its history. Second No. 11 (BWe 1920) came to Cornwall in 1950 from the Omaha, Lincoln & Beatrice RR in Nebraska. Two years after this photograph was taken in Cornwall on September 28th 1970, and following the CSR's abandonment of electric rail service, this unit found a home at the Ohio Railway Museum in Worthington, Ohio. (Omer Lavallée)

Below: The date is March 13th 1949, as the CSR's locomotive Third No.10 BWe 1921) switches the Howard Smith plant in Cornwall's west end. Prior to 1943 the locomotive had been No. 51 of the Washington & Old Dominion RR in Arlington, Virginia. (Omer Lavallée)

Above: While a Toronto-bound CN passenger train, headed by CN U-2 class 4-8-4 No. 6204, stops at the former Cornwall station on February 5th 1950, CSR's third locomotive No. 10 passes on the trolley spur. CSR trackage had been laid alongside the Canadian National line early in 1950 to replace trackage in paved city streets, which was abandoned after the Cornwall line ceased rail passenger service in 1949. (Anthony Clegg)

Below: An unidentified CSR locomotive, believed to be No. 14, hauls two boxcars along Water Street under the new international highway bridge, during the latter days of electric freight operations in the 1960s. (Cornwall Electric Archives)

Above: CSR's first locomotive assigned the number 9, builder unknown, was obtained from the Windsor, Essex and Lake Shore Rapid Railway in 1942. It is shown switching a hopper car at Cumberland and Second streets on June 29th 1943. Number 9 ended its days as a diesel electric locomotive at Bienfait, Saskatchewan. It can be seen in its reincarnation on page 81. (Anthony Clegg)

It simply isn't possible to run a transit system without a few mishaps. An accident report form (see page 56) was surely filled out to describe the situations captured on film, as shown here.

Left: This tram was in a collision with a truck.
(Charles P. DeRochie)

Below: This boxcar was pushed too far beyond the end-of-track, and was pushed right off its leading truck.
(Ronald S. Ritchie)

# SECTION ELEVEN

# Last Day Ceremony

THE cessation of this service was not destined to pass unnoticed. A number of interested people from Cornwall and Ottawa prevailed upon Canadian National to hold an official "last-day" ceremony. This occurred on an appropriately-rainy Saturday, October 9th 1971, when a convoy consisting of locomotive No. 14, CSR stationwagon No. E21, sweeper No. B1, CN International "Travelall" Hy-Rail No. TC 100, locomotives Nos. 16 and 15, line car No. 5, track maintenance car No. 4 and locomotive No. 17, operated from William Street to the old CN station via Marlborough, Water, Cumberland and Ninth streets. The parade, from the site of the old Canada mill of Canadian Cottons, was led by the Girls' Band of the North End Social Club, who boarded car No. 4 at Cumberland and Ninth for the remainder of the trip. At the old CN station, plow No. 3152, CN's "billboard" freight cars and a new caboose were on display.[71]

Concurrently, a complimentary shuttle service was offered for citizens from the old CN station area to Courtaulds' mill via the old northeastern loop line, using CN commuter coach No. 4997 pulled by CSR electric locomotive No. 7. More than seven hundred passengers were carried over the five hours during which this service was in operation.

At 16:00 (4 pm) that afternoon, CN Rideau Area manager George Van de Water presided at a series of speeches which paid tribute to the CSR's long and honorable service to the community. At its conclusion, he presented service car No. 4 and locomotive No. 17 to the City of Cornwall, to be preserved for historical purposes.[72] Domtar, the successor to Howard Smith paper mills, kindly agreed to store the vehicles at its Cornwall plant until a permanent location could be found. The preservation plan, however, hit a snag; during the following ten years, the vehicles were shunted from one siding to another on Domtar's property.

Finally, in 1981, Cornwall Electric, the Chamber of Commerce and the City of Cornwall arranged for the cosmetic restoration of the forty-ton locomotive and its exhibition in front of the Cornwall filtration plant. Unfortunately, No. 4, formerly tram No. 31 which had served in Fort Worth, Texas, then in Cornwall, was in very poor condition and was scrapped.[73]

Subsequent sales or donations of Cornwall equipment to various trolley museums saw locomotive No. 14 sent to the Illinois Railway Museum at Union, Illinois; locomotive No. 12 and plow No. 3152 were purchased by the Branford Electric Railway at East Haven, Connecticut; sweeper No. B2 went to the Seashore Trolley Museum at Kennebunkport, Maine; locomotive No. 11 was acquired by the Ohio Electric Railway Museum at Worthington, Ohio;

and locomotive No. 16 found a home at the Ontario Electric Railway Historical Association's museum near Rockwood, Ontario. Plow No. B1 and line car No. 5 were scrapped for parts by the National Museum of Science and Technology at Ottawa.

When the electrification was removed, CN lifted both the ex-CSR and its own old main line (ex GT) level crossings at Pitt Street, thus dividing the former CSR freight belt line into two portions. The western section, now left with no outside track connection, was reconnected with the new CN Montreal-Toronto main line by laying new track along the former Ottawa & New York roadbed to a new interchange.[74]

Below: The announcement for the Last Day Ceremonies and the parade of electric railway equipment, October 7th 1971. Copies of this flyer were distributed throughout the Cornwall area and attracted many citizens to the sombre event.

**PARADE**
Saturday, October 9th 1971
**CORNWALL, ONTARIO**
Canada's Last Common Carrier
Electric Railway
*SEE ELECTRIC EQUIPMENT & CN RAILWAY EQUIPMENT*
DEPARTS William St. at 9:00 am
via Water & Cumberland to Display Area
at NINTH & SYDNEY Sts.
▸ ▸ ▸ ▸ **FEATURING** ◂ ◂ ◂ ◂
*Rides behind an Eletric Locomotive*
Leaving at frequent intervals from the Brookdale Shopping Plaza to the Eastcourt Mall between 11 am & 4 pm.
*DETAILS FROM:* Joseph Tothfaluse 1(613)932-1430
Century Motel
Cornwall, Ontario
CHARBONNEAU THE PRINTER LTD. CORNWALL. ONT.

The result of the former CSR relinquishing service to Cornwall's industries resulted in at least three of these acquiring their own power for intra-plant switching in subsequent years. Canadian Industries Limited acquired such a unit as early as 1962. Combustion Engineering followed suit in 1973, while Courtaulds purchased Alco-built former CP Rail 1000 hp switcher No. 7096 in 1984.[75]

Now, a few decades later, a world facing diminishing oil supplies is actively pursuing applications of other forms of energy. The cleanliness, availability and flexibility of electricity for transportation purposes resulted in the retention of electric cars in Toronto, which courageously resisted the siren song of bus substitution put forward by automotive manufacturers in the 1940s and 1950s. The same factors have resulted, in the last decade, in the introduction of modernized streetcars (the new term is "LRV" for "light rail vehicle") not only on the existing rail system in Toronto, but on newly-built rail systems in two other Canadian cities (Calgary and Edmonton, Alberta.) in addition to many US ones. Concurrently, new LRV applications are being studied in a number of other North American communities.

Was Cornwall's electrification discarded too soon ? Only time will tell.

Top: The final parade of Cornwall electric equipment was led by the Girls' Band of the North End Social Club. (Ted Wickson)

Middle: CSR locomotive No. 14, part of the parade of CSR units that participated in the last run of electric railway equipment in Cornwall on October 9th 1971. (Ted Wickson)

Below: Locomotive No. 7 and the CN coach, with a crowd of potential passengers awaiting rides on the last day of CN-CSR electric freight operations, October 9th 1971.
(C. Robert Craig, C. Robert Craig Memorial Library, C2- CS1782)

Opposite top: CSR locomotive Second No. 17, being placed on display in front of the Cornwall filtration plant in August 1981.
(Cornwall Electric Archives)

Opposite bottom: Another view of Canadian National coach 4997, hauled by CSR electric locomotive No. 7, carrying passengers between the old CN station and the Courtaulds plant. (Ted Wickson)

Above: CSR No. 32 on the Belt Line route, turning from Pitt Street west onto Water Street, on April 18th 1948. (Allan Toohey)

Below: CSR 34, formerly Wilkes Barre Railways No. 344, was one of the reliable trams that provided Cornwall residents with efficient transit during the last days of Sun Life CSR ownership. (John D. Knowles)

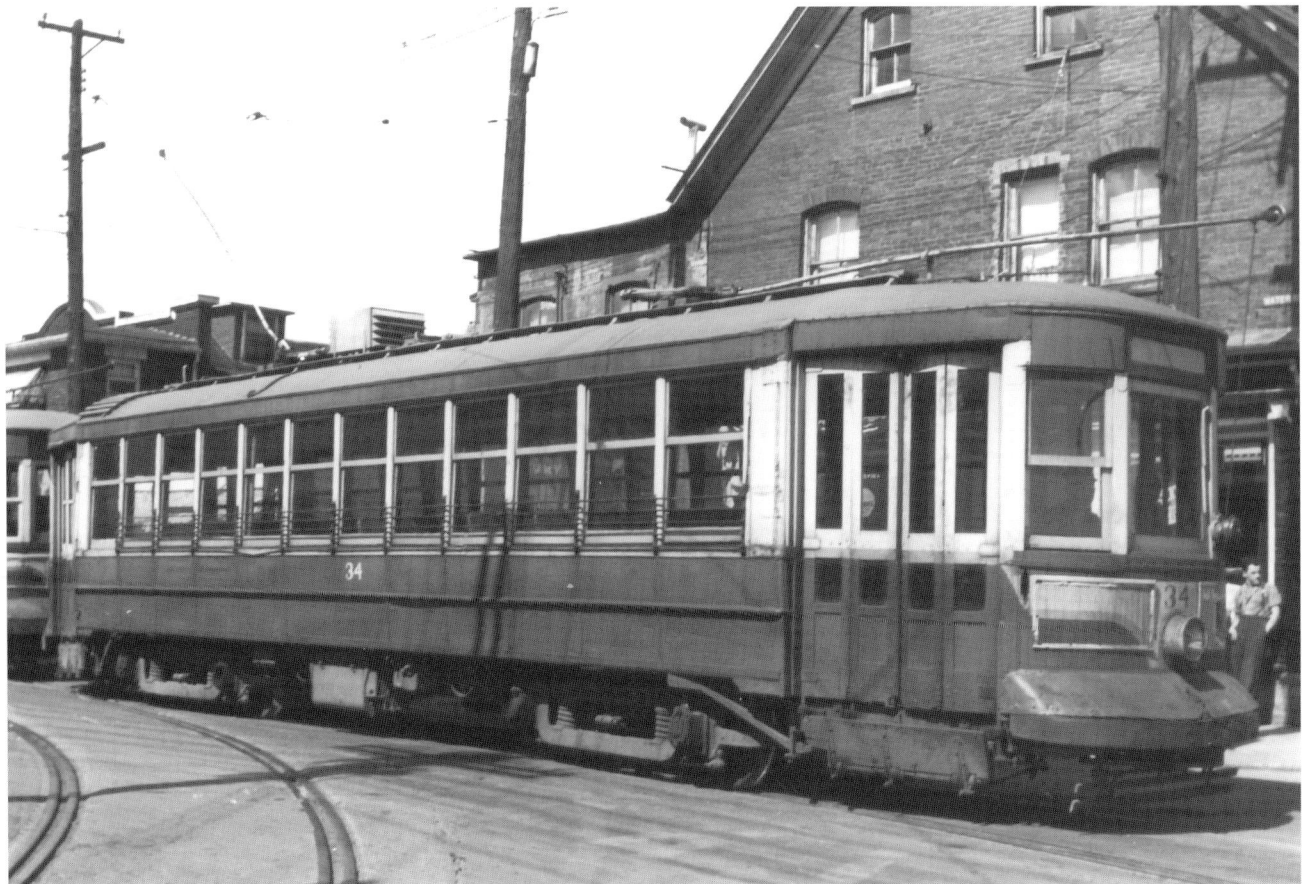

Above: CSR locomotives 8 and 12 on the freight-only line in eastern Cornwall, built to serve the Courtaulds rayon plant and other industries in Cornwall's east end. CSR 8 was formerly Aroostook Valley Railway No. 54. CSR 12 was from the Utah-Idaho Central, their No. 904. The former went to the scrapyards in 1971, while No. 12 went to the Shoreline Trolley Museum, Short Beach, Connecticut when CSR switching facilities were closed in 1971. (Ted Wickson)

Below: Western Dominion Coal Mines 3070, photographed March 23rd 1964 shortly after the colliery at Bienfait, Saskatchewan ceased operations. The diesel switcher had previously been Cornwall Street Railway Second No. 9, and was rebuilt when it was no longer required by the Cornwall system. It continued to provide service to several different corporate owners into the 21st century. (R. J. Sandusky)

Above: CSR 29, on one of its final railfan excursions on September 24th 1950. After cessation of regular rail passenger service in July, 1949, the unit was operated by the Cornwall Electric Railway Association on numerous excursions over the freight-only lines of the Cornwall system. (Omer Lavallée)

Below: Girls of the North End Social Club band board CSR No. 4 for the final leg of the commemorative parade, October 9th 1971, marking the end of Cornwall's freight switching services in the eastern Ontario community. Track maintenance car 4 had previously been passenger car 31, a mate of CSR 29, shown in the photo above. (Ted Wickson)

Above: The CSR's Fourth No. 1 was a double-truck steel locomotive-type snow sweeper, built by Ottawa in 1918 and acquired by Cornwall from the Hull Electric Railway when the latter was abandoned in 1947. Here it is shown "doing its thing", removing the snow from in front of the CSR carbarn, March 13th 1949. (Allan Toohey)

Below: CSR No. 28, formerly Jamestown Street Railway (Jamestown, New York), No. 86. Three cars, Jamestown No. 78, No. 84 and No. 86, had been purchased by Cornwall in 1938 and lasted until the cessation of CSR tram service in 1949. Photo of No. 28 taken soon after acquisition by Cornwall. (Al Paterson collection)

# SECTION TWELVE-A

# Roster of Rolling Stock

THE final section of this publication gives more factual and technical details on the items of rolling stock which served the Cornwall Street Railway over the seventy-five years of its existence in the transit field. The statistics are shown on Pages 85 and 87 in twelve columns.

The first three columns show the builder of the unit, the date built and construction number (where known). Columns 4 to 6 show the history of the unit before arriving in Cornwall. Columns 7 and 8 indicate the CSR numbers and a brief description of each car's use in Cornwall. Columns 9 to 11 show the disposal of the various items. Column 12 lists any special features and the page in this volume where the unit is illustrated.

The numbers shown in Column 7 indicate both the designation of the CSR unit and the frequency in the use of that number.

viz: 4/1 indicates the fourth unit to carry the number 1; 2/14 indicates the second unit to carry the number 14. In cases where the road number was used only once, the 1/ indication is omitted.

Abbreviations and contractions are explained on page 86.

Trolleycoach information is on page 92.

Description:
| | |
|---|---|
| Brny: | Birney Safety Car. |
| Clos: | Closed passenger car. |
| DE: | Double-end control. |
| DT: | Double truck. |
| Line: | Line car. |
| Loco: | Locomotive. |
| Open: | Open passenger car. |
| Plow: | Snow plow. |
| S: | Steel construction. |
| SE: | Single-end control. |
| ST: | Single truck. |
| Swpr: | Sweeper. |
| Towr: | Tower car. |
| Trk: | Track maintenance car. |
| W: | Wood construction. |
| X: | Scrapped |

Notes:

a: Possibly the four cars listed in *Poor's Manual* for the original line, inherited and used as trailers. Numbers assumed to integrate with new electric cars commencing at No. 5.

b: 2/#1 is commonly documented as ex-MSR #1 built by the Toronto Railway Co. in 1892. However, R.M. Binns, in *Montreal's Electric Streetcars*, records MSR #1 as scrapped in 1919. Hence, builder and origin of CSR 2/#1 is uncertain.

c: While commonly documented as ex-MP&IRy #33, it is presumed that 2/#2 was ex-MSR #33, formerly MP&I #13 in 1901. From R.M. Binns' book referred to above, MSR #34 was off the roster by 1907 but the other two mating cars, MSR #34 and #35 (ex-MP&I #14 and #15) remained on strength.

d: 2/#3, 3/#10 were disposed of by the CSR prior to January 1st 1971.

e: 3/#4 was acquired by Canadian National (CN) on January 1st 1971 and donated to the City of Cornwall for preservation on November 12th 1971 but was scrapped in 1981 due to deterioration.

f: 2/#5 was built using truck from a #42-47 series car, possibly #42. Replaced by 3/#4.

g: 3/#5 acquired by CN January 1st 1971. Offered to NMST, Ottawa (in lieu of #3152) in September 1972. Received October 1972 but broken up for display parts in November 1973.

h: 2/#6, 3/#7, 3/#8, 3/#9 and 2/#15 acquired by CN on January 1st 1971. Sold for scrap to St. Lawrence Iron & Metal Co. (SLI&M) on June 12th 1973.

i: 2/#7 said to have been built by the MSR for the Shawinigan Falls Terminal Railway, Shawinigan Falls, Quebec, as SFTR #1. Retired in 1908 and sold to the NST as its #7 in 1912. Retired in 1928 and sold to CSR in 1932.
- Other sources say that it was built by NST in 1905, sold to an equipment dealer in 1928 and sold to CSR in 1931. However, it is mounted on MSR trucks.
- Acquired by CRM on November 22nd 1959 from Courtaulds.

ii: Rebuilt from locomotive, Second No. 8 to snow plow with an air-operated steel plough, supplied by Ottawa Car and Aircraft Co.

j: 2/#9 was originally NST #12. Body sold to WEL to become that company's #9.
- After sale by CSR to AAM (as AAM #9), rebuilt into a diesel-electric locomotive and sold to Western Dominion Collieries, Bienfait, Saskatchewan, as WDC #3070.

k: 2/#10 was originally WEL #50 (express motor), rebuilt as WEL #10 (locomotive) in 1930.
- Scrapped for parts upon acquisition by CSR.

l: 1/#11 is usually recorded as constructed by an unknown builder, possibly NST, as NST #11.
- Other sources have related this unit to be ex-Chatham, Wallaceburg & Lake Erie Railway (CW&LE) #20 (ex-Brooklyn Dock in 1908), said sold to CSR in 1928 but cannot be verified from photos. Where abouts of CW&LE #20 is unknown.

m: OLB #2 originally built for Youngstown & Ohio River RR #7, acquired by OLB in 1933. Acquired by CN on January 1st 1971. Sold to Ohio Railway Museum on June 1st 1972.

n: NJR #11 originally built for Chicago, South Shore & South Bend RR as CSS&SB #1005. CSS&SB Nos. 1005-1006 acquired by NJR as Nos. 11 and 10 in December 1941.
Scrapped for parts by CSR upon acquisition.

This roster of rolling stock is followed by three chronological summaries; one showing the unit numbers carried by the passenger vehicles on the CSR, another showing the acquisition and disposal of the electric locomotives that served the city's industries, and a third giving an explanation of the use and re-use of numbers 1 to 5, designating the snow-fighting and work equipment on the Cornwall system.

| 1 | 2 | 3 | 4 | 5 | 6 | 7 | 8 | 9 | 10 | 11 | | 12 |
|---|---|---|---|---|---|---|---|---|---|---|---|---|
| Origin | | | Prior | | | Roster | | Disposal | | | Note | Photo |
| Bldr | MM-YY | C/N | Co. | No. | MM-YY | No. | Desc. | MM-YY | In | No. | | |
| CGE? | - | | | | -96 | **1/1** | **Clos** | ? | ? | | a | |
| TRC | -92 | | MSR | 1 | -99 | **2/1** | **Swpr ST DE W** | -30 | x | | b | 6 |
| LAR | -97 | | CSR | 2/2 | -30 | **3/1** | **Swpr ST DE W** | -47 | x | | | |
| OTT | -18 | | HER | 106 | -47 | **4/1** | **Swpr DT DE S** | -59 | x | | | 42,83,98,101 |
| CGE? | - | | | | -96 | **1/2** | **Clos** | ? | ? | | a | |
| LAR | -97 | | MPI | 33 | -05 | **2/2** | **Swpr DT DE W** | -30 | CSR | 3/1 | c | |
| McG | -97 | | KPC | 2 | -30 | **3/2** | **Swpr ST DE W** | -48 | x | | | 42,43 |
| CGE? | - | | | | -96 | **1/3** | **Clos** | ? | ? | | a | |
| McG | - | | WR | ? | -34 | **2/3** | **Swpr ST DE W** | -71 | x | | d | |
| CGE? | - | | | | -96 | **1/4** | **Clos** | ? | ? | | a | |
| BWe | -99 | | CSR | 1/12 | -30 | **2/4** | **Plow DT DE W** | -48 | x | | | 89 |
| StL | -27 | | CSR | 31 | -50 | **3/4** | **Trk DT DE S** | -71 | x | | e | 82,86 |
| TRy | -96 | | | | new | **1/5** | **Open ST DE W** | -16 | CSR | 42 | | 18,19 |
| CSR | -34 | | | | new | **2/5** | **Towr ST DE W** | -50 | x | | f | 62 |
| StL | -27 | | CER | 29 | -52 | **3/5** | **Line DT SE S** | -71 | x | | g | 62 |
| TRy | -96 | | | | new | **1/6** | **Clos ST DE W** | -16 | CSR | 45 | | |
| BWe | 12-19 | 52703 | KCK | 502 | -44 | **2/6** | **Loco DT DE S** | -71 | x | | h | 72,73,96 |
| TRy | -96 | | | | new | **1/7** | **Open ST DE W** | -16 | CSR | 43 | | 20 |
| MSR | -99 | | NST | 7 | -32 | **2/7** | **Loco DT SE S** | -46 | CRT | 7 | i | 21,98,101 |
| BWe | 12-23 | 57557 | STR | 15 | 12/56 | **3/7** | **Loco DT SE S** | -71 | x | | h | 78,79 |
| TRy | -96 | | | | new | **1/8** | **Clos ST DE W** | -16 | CSR | 46 | | |
| NST | -24 | | NST | 10 | -34 | **2/8** | **Loco DT SE S** | -46 | CSR | P-8 | ii | 24 |
| BWe | 10-24 | 58023 | AVR | 54 | 8/46 | **3/8** | **Loco DT SE S** | -71 | x | | h | 5,81,98 |
| TRy | -96 | | | | new | **1/9** | **Open ST DE W** | -16 | CSR | 44 | | 55 |
| ? | - | | WEL | 9 | -42 | **2/9** | **Loco DT DE S** | -52 | AAM | 9 | j | 5,59,60,70,76 |
| BWe | 5-13 | 39866 | NJC | 4 | -52 | **3/9** | **Loco DT DE S** | -71 | x | | h | |
| TRy | -96 | | | | new | **1/10** | **Clos ST DE W** | -16 | CSR | 47 | | 16 |
| WEL | -30 | | WEL | 10 | -42 | **2/10** | **Loco DT DE S** | -42 | x | | k | |
| BWe | 4-21 | 54704 | WOD | 51 | -43 | **3/10** | **Loco DT DE S** | -71 | x | | d | 73,74,75 |
| ? | ? | | NST | 11 | -28 | **1/11** | **Loco DT DE S** | -50 | x | | l | 70 |
| BWe | 10-20 | 53785 | OLB | 2 | -50 | **2/11** | **Loco DT DE S** | -71 | ORM | | m | 74 |
| BWe | -99 | | | | new | **1/12** | **Loco DT DE S** | -30 | CSR | 2/4 | | |
| Brl | -20 | | EPR | ? | -34 | **2/12** | **Brny ST DE S** | -48 | x | | | |
| BWe | 5-17 | 45657 | UIC | 904 | 4/48 | **3/12** | **Loco DT DE S** | -71 | BFD | | | 66,81,89 |
| Brl | -20 | | EPR | ? | -34 | **1/13** | **Brny ST DE S** | -47 | x | | | |
| BWe | 4-24 | 57715 | NJC | 11 | -52 | **2/13** | **Loco DT DE S** | -52 | | | n | |
| ? | ? | | OER | ? | -98 | **1/14** | **Clos ST DE W** | -20 | x | | | |
| Brl | -20 | | EPR | ? | -34 | **2/14** | **Brny ST DE S** | -41 | LTC | 102 | | 48 |
| BWe | 1-29 | 6701 | STR | 20 | 12/56 | **3/14** | **Loco DT DE S** | -71 | x | | | 51,78 |

## Builder's Initials:

| | |
|---|---|
| Brl | J.G. Brill Co., Philadelphia, Pennsylvania |
| BWe | Baldwin-Westinghouse, Philadelphia, Pennsylvania |
| CCF | Canadian Car & Foundry Ltd., Montreal, Quebec |
| CGE | Canadian General Electric, Peterborough, Ontario |
| CSR | Cornwall Street Railway, Light & Power Co. |
| EMS | Eastern Massachusetts Street Ry. Co., Boston, Massachusetts |
| Kuh | G.C. Kuhlman Car Co., Cleveland, Ohio |
| LAR | N. and A.C. Lariviere, Montreal, Quebec |
| McG | McGuire-Cummings Co., Paris, Illinois |
| MSR | Montreal Street Railway Co., Montreal, Quebec |
| NST | Niagara, St. Catharines & Toronto Ry. Co., St. Catharines, Ontario |
| Ott | Ottawa Car Manufacturing Co., Ottawa, Ontario |
| StL | St. Louis Car Company, St. Louis, Missouri |
| TRy | Toronto Railway Co., Toronto, Ontario |
| WEL | Windsor, Essex & Lake Shore Rapid Ry. Co., Windsor, Ontario |

## Owner's Initials:

| | |
|---|---|
| AAM | Andrew Merrilees Ltd., Toronto, Ontario (dealer) |
| AVR | Aroostook Valley RR Co., Presque Isle, Maine |
| BER | Boston Elevated Railroad Co., Boston, Massachusetts |
| BFD | Branford Electric Railway Ass'n, now Shoreline Trolley Museum, Short Beach, Connecticut |
| CER | Cornwall Electric Railway Society (museum) |
| CRM | Canadian Railway Museum, Delson/St-Constant, Quebec |
| CRT | Courtaulds (Canada) Ltd., Cornwall, Ontario |
| CSR | Cornwall Street Railway, Light & Power Co., Cornwall, Ontario |
| EMS | Eastern Massachusetts Street Railway Co., Boston, Massachusetts |
| EPR | Eastern Pennsylvania Rys., Pottsville, Pennsylvania |
| FST | Fairchance & Smithfield Traction Co., Uniontown, Pennsylvania |

| | |
|---|---|
| GRR | Grand River Railway Co., Preston, Ontario |
| HER | Hull Electric Railway Co., Hull, Quebec |
| IRM | Illinois Railway Museum, Union, Illinois |
| ISC | Indiana Service Corp., Fort Wayne, Indiana |
| JSR | Jamestown Street Railway Co., Jamestown, New York |
| KCK | Kansas City, Kaw Valley & Western Ry., Kansas City, Kansas. |
| KPC | Kingston, Portsmouth & Cataraqui Ry. Co., Kingston, Ontario |
| LEN | Lake Erie & Northern Ry. Co., Preston, Ontario |
| LTC | Levis Tramways Co., Levis, Quebec |
| MPI | Montreal Park & Island Ry. Co., Montreal, Quebec |
| MSR | Montreal Street Railway Co., Montreal, Quebec |
| MTC | Montreal Tramways Company, Montreal, Quebec |
| NJR | Niagara Junction Ry. Co., Niagara Falls, New York |
| NMS | National Museum of Science and Technology, Ottawa, Ontario |
| NST | Niagara, St. Catharines & Toronto Ry. Co., St. Catharines, Ontario |
| NTT | Northern Texas Traction Co., Fort Worth, Texas |
| NYC | New York City, Dept. of Plant and Structures, (Staten Island Midland Divn.), New York, New York |
| OER | Ottawa Electric Railway Co., Ottawa, Ontario |
| OHA | Ontario Electric Railway Historical Association, (Halton County Radial Ry.), Rockwood, Ontario |
| ORM | Ohio Electric Railway Museum, Worthington, Ohio |
| OLB | Omaha, Lincoln & Beatrice Railway Co., Lincoln, Nebraska |
| OTC | Ottawa Transportation Commission, Ottawa, Ontario |
| SEA | Seashore Electric Railway Museum, Kennebunkport, Maine |
| STH | St. Thomas Street Railway Co., St. Thomas, Ontario |
| STR | Springfield Terminal Ry. Co., Springfield, Vermont |
| TTC | Toronto Transportation Commission, Toronto, Ontario |
| UIC | Utah-Idaho Central Ry. Co., Ogden, Utah |
| URE | United Railways & Electric Co., Baltimore, Maryland |
| WBR | Wilkes-Barre Railways, Wilkes-Barre, Pennsylvania |
| WEL | Windsor, Essex & Lake Shore Rapid Ry. Co., Windsor, Ontario |

Below: The Girls' Band of the North End Social Club, which led the commemorative parade, boarded CSR car No. 4 at Cumberland and Ninth streets for the latter part of the trip around the city. (Ted Wickson)

Notes (continued):

o: 2/#16, #18, #20 ex-TTC Nos. 2216/30/34 were originally Toronto Civic Railways Nos. 60, 67, 69.

p: 3/#16 acquired by CN on January 1st 1971. Requested by NMS in August 1971 but request cancelled in September 1972 due to condition. Sold to OHA June 6th 1973.

q: 1/#17 retired in March 1947 and converted to paint storage car in August 1947. Scrapped in January 1949.

r: 2/#17 acquired by CN on January 1st 1971. Donated to City of Cornwall on November 12th 1971 and stored at Domtar Paper Mills. Restored for the Cornwall Chamber of Commerce (under the direction of D.R. Seymour, retired assistant general manager of CSR) and moved to a display site on Second Street beside the CSR (CN) right-of-way in August 1981. Plaque installed in June 1983.

s: Former WPS number for #23 is unknown. However, Birney cars in WPS fleet were built in 1920, 1921 and 1922.

t: #25 painted black with moons, stars, clock and other nocturnal symbols with "Father Time" riding in a stand on the roof, for the ceremonial last run on July 27th 1949.

u: 1/#26 was reported to have been acquired in 1900 or 1901. It was sold to the Magee Museum, Bloomsburg, Pennsylvania, by Courtaulds after 1971.

v: #29 donated to the Cornwall Electric Railway Society (CER) in 1949 and used for fantrips in 1949-50. Returned to CSR and rebuilt as 3/#5 (tower car) in 1952. Not preserved.

w: Nos. 29, 30, 31, 2/32 ex-Northern Texas Traction Co., Fort-Worth, Texas, 250 series cars.

ww: Nos. 36, 38 were the first double-truck cars purchased by the CSR. They were equipped with maximum traction trucks.

x: Scrapped

y: #3152 replaced P-8 and was assigned new number 8P but not repainted. It was requested by the NMS in August 1971 but the request was cancelled in September of that year. 3/#5 was substituted in September 1972. #3152 was sold to Branford in 1972.

z: #B1 was assigned number "1" but not repainted. Requested by NMS in August 1971 and delivered in October 1972.

aa: #B2 was assigned number "10" but not repainted. Sold to Seashore Trolley Museum in June 1972.

bb: #E10, ex BER #E-10, was originally EMS #E-10, rebuilt in 1920 from express motor E-10 built in 1909.

cc: 2/#24 out of service in March 1947.

dd: 2/#32 accidentally burned in April 1944. Rebuilt, scrapped in 1949

| 1 | 2 | 3 | 4 | 5 | 6 | 7 | 8 | 9 | 10 | 11 | Note | Photo |
|---|---|---|---|---|---|---|---|---|---|---|---|---|
| Origin | | | Prior | | | Roster | | Disposal | | | | |
| Bldr | MM-YY | C/N | Co. | No. | MM-YY | No. | Desc. | MM-YY | In | No. | Note | Photo |
| Brl | -20 | | NYC | ? | -28 | **1/15** | **Brny ST DE S** | 8-48 | x | | | 32 |
| BWe | 9/15 | 42474 | LEN | 333 | 6-62 | **2/15** | **Loco DT DE S** | -71 | x | | h | |
| ? | ? | | OER | ? | -98 | **1/16** | **Clos ST DE W** | -20 | x | | | 18 |
| Brl | -20 | | TTC | 2216 | 5-27 | **2/16** | **Brny ST DE S** | -47 | x | | o | 25 |
| BWe | 9/15 | 42475 | LEN | 335 | 6-62 | **3/16** | **Loco DT DE S** | -71 | x | | p | |
| Brl | -20 | | URE | 4031 | 6-28 | **1/17** | **Brny ST DE S** | 8-49 | x | | q | 28 |
| BWe | 8/30 | 61456 | GRR | 230 | 11-62 | **2/17** | **Loco DT DE S** | -71 | Cornwall | | r | 79,ibc |
| Brl | 7/20 | | TTC | 2230 | 5-27 | **18** | **Brny ST DE S** | 4-49 | x | | o | 26,29,96 |
| Brl | -20 | | URE | 4033 | 6-28 | **19** | **Brny ST DE S** | 8-48 | x | | | 94 |
| Brl | 7/20 | | TTC | 2234 | 5-27 | **20** | **Brny ST DE S** | -47 | x | | o | 31 |
| Brl | -21 | | FST | 103 | -29 | **21** | **Brny ST DE S** | -41 | LTC | 101 | | 49 |
| Brl | -94 | | MSR | 222 | -07 | **1/22** | **Clos ST DE W** | -16 | CSR | 32 | | |
| Brl | -23 | | FST | 104 | -29 | **2/22** | **Brny ST DE S** | 8-48 | x | | | |
| StL | -21 | | WPS | XX | -30 | **23** | **Brny ST DE S** | -42 | LTC | 103 | s | 46 |
| Brl | -94 | | MSR | 224 | -07 | **1/24** | **Clos ST DE W** | -16 | CSR | 34 | | |
| StL | -21 | | WPS | X37 | -30 | **2/24** | **Brny ST DE S** | 8-48 | x | | cc | 26 |
| Brl | -22 | | EMS | 6014 | -37 | **25** | **Clos DT DE S** | -49 | x | | t | 2,12,34,40,41 |
| BWe | -99 | | | | new | **1/26** | **Loco DT DE W** | -32 | CRT | 26 | u | 16, 27 |
| StL | -17 | | JSR | 78 | -38 | **2/26** | **Clos DT DE S** | -49 | x | | | 38,97 |
| StL | -17 | | JSR | 84 | -38 | **27** | **Clos DT DE S** | -49 | x | | | |
| StL | -17 | | JSR | 86 | -38 | **28** | **Clos DT DE S** | -49 | x | | | 39,49,58,83,94,97,102 |
| StL | -30 | | NTT | ? | -39 | **29** | **Clos DT DE S** | -49 | CER/CSR | | w | 56,58-61,82,92 |
| StL | -30 | | NTT | ? | -39 | **30** | **Clos DT DE S** | -49 | x | | w | 30,38,39 |
| StL | -30 | | NTT | ? | -39 | **31** | **Clos DT DE S** | -50 | CSR | 3/4 | w | 3,13,36 |
| Brl | -94 | | CSR | 1/22 | -16 | **1/32** | **Clos ST DE W** | -28 | x | | w | |
| StL | -30 | | NTT | ? | -39 | **2/32** | **Clos DT DE S** | 4-49 | x | | dd | 4,80,88 |
| StL | -17 | | ISC | 508 | -45 | **33** | **Clos DT DE S** | -49 | x | | | 39,49,98,99 |
| Brl | -94 | | CSR | 1/24 | -16 | **1/34** | **Clos ST DE W** | -28 | x | | | |
| Brl | -11 | | WBR | 344 | -42 | **2/34** | **Clos DT DE W** | -49 | x | | | 37,80,94 |
| Brl | -11 | | WBR | 350 | -42 | **35** | **Clos DT DE W** | -49 | x | | | 34,42 |
| Kuh | -11 | | STh | ? | -26 | **36** | **Clos DT DE W** | -49 | x | | ww | 35,50 |
| StL | -23 | | ISC | 516 | -45 | **37** | **Clos DT DE S** | -49 | x | | | 12,38,46,47,88 |
| Kuh | -11 | | STh | ? | -26 | **38** | **Clos DT DE W** | -49 | x | | ww | 32 |
| TRy | -96 | | CSR | 1/5 | -16 | **42** | **Clos ST DE W** | -28 | x | | | |
| TRy | -96 | | CSR | 1/7 | -16 | **43** | **Clos ST DE W** | -27 | x | | | |
| TRy | -96 | | CSR | 1/9 | -16 | **44** | **Clos ST DE W** | -27 | x | | | |
| TRy | -96 | | CSR | 1/6 | -16 | **45** | **Clos ST DE W** | -30 | x | | | |
| TRy | -96 | | CSR | 1/8 | -16 | **46** | **Clos ST DE W** | -28 | x | | | |
| TRy | -96 | | CSR | 1/10 | -16 | **47** | **Clos ST DE W** | -29 | x | | | |
| CCF | -25 | | MTC | 3152 | -57 | **3152** | **Plow DT SE S** | -71 | BFD | | y | 50 |
| Ott | -26 | | OTC | B1 | -59 | **B1** | **Swpr ST DE W** | -71 | NMS | | z | ifc |
| Ott | -26 | | OTC | B2 | -59 | **B2** | **Swpr ST DE W** | -71 | SEA | | aa | 51 |
| EMS | -09 | | BER | E10 | -45 | **E10** | **Swpr DT DE W** | -57 | x | | bb | 43,47 |
| NST | -24 | | CSR | 2/8 | -46 | **P8** | **Plow DT SE S** | -58 | x | | | |

# SECTION TWELVE-B

## Quick Reference

The combined roster of Cornwall Street Railway equipment shown on pages 85 and 87, accurate though it may be, is rather difficult to follow. The following divisions of the listing are more understandable.

Below, top: Single-truck Birney cars await their assignments in front of the CSR carbarn. (John D. Knowles)

Middle: "The Toonerville Trolley That Meets All The Trains", a popular contemporary feature by cartoonist Fontaine Fox, is the theme for this photo of CSR No. 32 at the CN train station, taken from the coach window of a moving train bound for Montreal on August 25th 1946. (Anthony Clegg)

Bottom: CSR No. 37 travels along the side-of-road trackage to the New York Central station on Second Street West, in this view recorded on October 14th 1947. No. 37 was received from Indiana Service Corp. in Fort Wayne in 1945. (Allan Toohey, CRHA collection)

### a. Quick Reference Index

Service cars (15)

| 2/1 | 2/5 | 42474 |
|---|---|---|
| 3/1 re# | 3/5 conv. CN* (g) | |
| 4/1 | E-10 (bb) | |
| 2/2 | B-1 CN (z) | 42475 |
| 3/2 | B-2 CN* (aa) | |
| 2/3 | 3152 (y) | 61456 |
| 2/4 conv. | P8 conv. | |
| 3/4 CN* | | |

Locomotives (19)

| 2/6 CN* | 2/10 | 3/14 CN (d) |
|---|---|---|
| 2/7 | 3/10 (d) | 2/15 CN* |
| 3/7 CN* | 1/11 | 3/16 CN* |
| 2/8 | 2/11 CN* | 2/17 CN* (r) |
| 3/8 CN* | 1/12 | 1/26 (u) |
| 2/9 | 3/12 CN* | |
| 3/9 CN* | 2/13 | |

Single Truck Wood Passenger cars (18+4?)

| 1/1 | 1/9 | 42 re# |
|---|---|---|
| 1/2 | 1/10 | 43 re# |
| 1/3 | 1/14 | 44 re# |
| 1/4 | 1/16 | 45 re# |
| 1/5 | 1/22 | 46 re# |
| 1/6 | 1/24 | 47 re# |
| 1/7 | 1/32 re# | |
| 1/8 | 1/34 re# | |

Single Truck Birney Safety cars (13)

| 2/12 | 1/17 (g) | 2/22 |
|---|---|---|
| 1/13 | 18 | 23 (s) |
| 2/14 | 19 | 2/24 |
| 1/15 | 20 (o) | |
| 2/16 (o) | 21 | |

Double Truck Passenger cars (14)

| 25 (t) | 30 | 35 |
|---|---|---|
| 2/26 | 31 | 36 |
| 27 | 2/32 | 37 |
| 28 | 33 | 38 |
| 29 (v) | 2/34 | |

### b. Equipment Acquired by Canadian National (January 1st 1971)

Locomotives

| 2/6 (h) | 3/12 | |
|---|---|---|
| 3/7 (h) | 3/14 | |
| 3/8 (h) | 2/15 (h) | |
| 3/9 (h) | 3/16 (p) | |
| 2/11 | 2/17 | |

Works Equipment

| B/1 (1) Sweeper (z) | |
|---|---|
| B/2 (10) Sweeper (aa) | |
| 3/4 Track Maintenance Car (e) | |
| 3/5 Line Car (g) | |
| 3152 (8P) Plow (y) | |

Notes: CN: To CN, January 1st 1971.
* : In final parade.
§ : Disposal mentioned in text.

# ALL TWELVES

Top left: CSR logo, photographed on the side of locomotive 12. Similar identification was applied to other equipment during the latter days of Sun Life transit operations in Cornwall. (C. Robert Craig, C. Robert Craig Memorial Library, C2-CS1427)

Top right: Cornwall's First No. 12 was a Baldwin-Westinghouse locomotive with a wooden cab, built in 1899. It was rebuilt as a snow-plow, and renumbered Second No. 4 in 1930. (Charles P. DeRochie)

Middle: In 1934, CSR filled the No. 12 designation with a Birney, purchased from the Eastern Pennsylvania Railways (Pottsville). It served the Cornwall system until 1948. (Charles P. DeRochie)

Bottom: CSR Third No. 12 was a locomotive purchased in 1948 from the Utah-Idaho Central RR, Ogden, Utah. In 1971 it went to the Branford Electric Railroad Museum at Short Beach, Connecticut. (Allan Toohey, CRHA collection)

# SECTION TWELVE-C

## Summary 1

THE identity of the items of rolling stock on the Cornwall Street Railway is rather difficult to follow, particularly the numbers asigned to the passenger trams. Unit numbers of the streetcars and the locomotives overlapped, and at times appeared to have been duplicated although this was not actually the case. The following is a simplified chronology of the numbers assigned to the passenger cars on the Cornwall system.

| YEAR | ACTIVITY - Purchase of cars, disposals, etc. | UNIT NUMBERS ADDED | UNIT NUMBERS DELETED |
|---|---|---|---|
| 1896 | Four cars from the steam dummy line | 1, 2, 3, 4 | 1, 2, 3, 4 |
| | Three open cars and three closed cars from Toronto Street Railway | 5, 6, 7, 8, 9, 10 | |
| 1898 | Two closed cars from Ottawa | 14, 16 | |
| 1907 | Two closed cars from Montreal | 22, 24 | |
| 1916 | Rebuilding and renumbering of Toronto cars | 42, 43, 44, 45, 46, 47 | 5, 6, 7, 8, 9, 10 |
| | Rebuilding and renumbering of Montreal cars | 32, 34 | 22, 24 |
| 1920 | Cars from Ottawa retired | | 14, 16 |
| 1926 | Two double truck cars from St. Thomas | 39, 38 | |
| 1927 | Three Birneys from TTC | 16, 18, 20 | |
| | Two older Toronto cars retired | | 43, 44 |
| 1928 | Three Birneys from USA | 15, 17, 19 | |
| | Four older cars retired, one rebuilt to Tower car 2/5 | | 32, 34, 42, 46 |
| 1929 | One older car retired | | 47 |
| 1930 | Four Birneys from USA | 21, 22, 23, 24 | |
| | Last of the older cars retired | | 45 |
| 1934 | Three Birney cars from USA | 12, 13, 14 | |
| 1937 | Double truck car from EMS, Boston | 25 | |
| 1938 | Three double truck cars from JSR | 26, 27, 28 | |
| 1939 | Four cars from Northern Teaxas Traction | 29, 30, 31, 32 | |
| 1941 | Two Birneys transferred to Levis by order of Cdn. Transit Controller | | 14, 21 |
| 1942 | Another Birney transferred to Levis, Quebec | 34, 35 | 23 |
| | Two cars reeceived from Wilkes-Barre, Pennsylvania | 34, 35 | |
| 1945 | Two cars from Indiana Service Commission, Fort Wayne, Indiana | 33, 37 | |
| 1947 | Three Birneys scrapped | | 13, 16, 20 |
| 1948 | Five Birneys scrapped | | 12, 15, 19, 22, 24 |
| **** | PASSENGER SERVICE DISCONTINUED IN 1949 | | |
| 1949 | Most remaining cars scrapped in 1949 except 29 and 31 | | 11, 18, 25, 26, 27, 28, 30, 32, 33, 34, 35, 36, 37, 38 |
| 1950 | 31 converted to 3rd 4 | | |
| 1952 | 29 converted to 3rd 5 | | |
| 1971 | Electric railway discontinued and all remaining units were disposed of, scrapped or sold. | | |

# Summary 2

The following is a simplified chronology of the identity of the Cornwall Street Railway locomotives.

| YEAR | ACTIVITY - Purchase of cars, disposals, etc. | UNIT NUMBERS ADDED | UNIT NUMBERS DELETED |
|------|----------------------------------------------|--------------------|-----------------------|
| 1899 | Locomotive 12 acquired new | 12 | |
| 1907 | Locomotive 26 acquired from unknown source | 26 | |
| 1926 | Locomotive 26 to Courtaulds | | 26 |
| 1928 | Locomotive 11 from NST | 11 | |
| 1930 | Locomotive 12 converted to plow 4 | | 12 |
| 1932 | Locomotive 7 acquired from NST 7 | 7 | |
| 1934 | Locomotive 8 from NST 10 | 8 | |
| 1942 | Locomotive 9 from WFL 9 (Windsor, Essex & Lake Shore) | 9 | 10 |
| | Locomotive 10 for parts | 10 | |
| 1943 | Locomotive 10 from WOD 51 (Washington & Old Dominion) | 10 | |
| 1944 | Locomotive 6 from Kansas City, Kaw Valley & Western 502 | 6 | |
| 1946 | Locomotive 8 from Aroostook Valley RR 54 | 8 | |
| | Locomotive 7 to Courtaulds 7 | | 7 (then to CRHA) |
| | Locomotive 8 converted to plow 8 | | 8 |
| 1948 | Locomotive 12 from Utah-Idaho Central 904 | 12 | |
| 1950 | Locomotive 11 fro Omaha, Lincoln & Beatrice 2 | 11 | old 11 |
| 1952 | Locomotive 9 from Niagara Junction 4 | 9 | old 9 |
| | Old locomotive 9 to AAM, then to WDS as diesel locomotive | | |
| 1956 | Locomotive 7 from Springfield Terminal 20 | 7 | |
| | Locomotive 13 from Niagara Junction 11 for parts | 13 | 13 (parts) |
| | Locomotive 14 from Springfield Terminal | 14 | |
| | Locomotive 15 from Lake Erie & Northern 333 | 15 | |
| | Locomotive 16 from Lake Erie & Northern 335 | 16 | |
| | Locomotive 17 from Grand River Ry. 230 | 17 | |

In 1971, when electric railway service in Cornwall was discontinued, the CSR had the following locomotives: 6, 7, 8, 9, 10, 11, 12, 14, 15, 16, 17.

DISPOSALS:
- Sold for scrap to SLI&M:        6, 7, 8, 9, 15
- Presumed scrapped by CSR:       10
- To Ohio Railway Museum:         11
- To Branford Railway Museum:     12 (South Shore Trolley Museum)
- To Illinois Railway Museum:     14
- To Ont. Elect. Rwy. Hist. Assoc.: 16 (Halton)
- Display at Cornwall, Ontario:   17

# Summary 3

Particularly difficult to follow, in an analysis of the numbering system on the Cornwall Street Railway, is the use of numbers between 1 and 5. Apart from the original 1 to 4, the presumed original passenger cars most likely inherited from the steam dummy system of 1896, and the First #5, one of the passenger units from Toronto, there were nine items of rolling stock with these five numbers, as outlined below:

2/1 a single-truck sweeper from 1899 to 1930, scrapped in 1930.

3/1 a single-truck sweeper from 1930 to 1947: this unit was previously 2/2.

4/1 a double-truck sweeper from Hull Electric Railway 106, which replaced 3/1 in 1947 and lasted until the year 1959.

2/2 was a sweeper from the turn of the century until 1930, when it was re-designated 3/1.

3/2 was a single-truck sweeper, built by McGuire Cummings, of Paris, Illinois, which operated from 1930 until the last winter of electrified rail passenger service in 1948.

2/3, also a single-truck McGuire Cummings sweeper from 1934 to 1971.

2/4 was double-truck plow built from locomotive 1/12 in 1930. It lasted until 1948. In 1950. the number 4 was again used when passenger car 31 was rebuilt into a track maintenance vehicle, the Third #4. This unit lasted until 1971.

2/5 was the tower car for the maintenance of the electrical overhead. It was built using a truck from a 43-47 series car (probably 42) and lasted until the early 1950s when it was replaced by double-truck tower car 3/5, which had been rebuilt from passenger car 29. This unit lasted until the end of electrified railway service in 1971.

The following are also to be mentioned on the list of work equipment after 1945:

E10 from Boston in 1945, scrapped in 1957

3152 from Montreal in 1957. It went to Branford in 1972.

P8 built from Locomotive 2/8, ex NS&T. Scrapped in 1958.

B1 and B2, which were received from Ottawa in 1959. These two single-truck sweepers lasted until cessation of service in 1971. B1 went to NMST in October, 1972, while B2 was sold to the Seashore Trolley Museum in June 1972.

# SECTION TWELVE-D

## Time-line summary for Cornwall Electric Transit Services

July 7th 1886........................First electric tram service
          1901........................First electric freight service
June 8th 1949......................Trolleycoach service started
July 27th 1949......................End of electric tram service
May 31st 1970......................End of trolleycoach service
April 1st 1971........................CN took control of system
August 7th 1971...................Last revenue freight service
October 9th 1971................Final ceremony

Below: An interior view of one of the Fort Worth cars. Padded leather-upholstered seats provided Cornwall patrons with superb comfort on their CSR travels. (Allan Toohey)

## Trolleycoaches operated by Cornwall Street Railway Light & Power Company

| ROAD NUMBERS | SERIAL NUMBERS | ORDERED | DELIVERED |
|---|---|---|---|
| 100 - 114 | 5550 - 5564 | March 1948 | Junuary 1949 |
| 115 | 5000 | Built as demonstrator, 1946 | Sold to CSR, Oct.-Nov. 1951 |

All CSR trolleycoaches were built by Canadian Car & Foundry, model T-44 with Canadian General Electric electrical equipment.

• Nos. 105, 109, 114, 115 :
  Scrapped prior to May 1970.

• Nos. 101, 103, 113 :
  Stored as of May 1970.
  Sold to TTC for spare parts in September 1970

• Nos. 100, 102, 104, 105, 106, 107, 108, 110, 111, 112 :
  Retired May 31st 1970. Sold to TTC for spare parts in September 1970.

# SECTION THIRTEEN

# Bibliography

1. Encyclopedia Canadiana (1975), vol. 3, pp. 18-119, "Cornwall".
2. *ibid.*
3. *ibid.*
4. *Serving Cornwall for 50 Years*, The Stormont Electric Light and Power Company Ltd.
5. Larmonth, J.H., Report on the Cornwall Street Railway Light and Power Company, Cornwall, Ontario, March 8th 1919. Typewritten memorandum. Canadian Pacific Corporate Archives (No. X88) Montreal.
6. *The Freeholder*, November 27th 1885.
7. DeRochie, Charles P., Cornwall Street Railway, Cornwall, Ontario, *50 Years of Continual Service*, 1896-1946 [privately printed] 1946.
8. *The Freeholder*, February 15th 1886.
9. *ibid.*, April 30th 1886.
10. *Poor's Manual of Railroads*, 1889, p.61 (appendix); *ibid.*, 1890, p.1242; ibid, 1891, p.1238.
11. Wilson, Donald M., *Lost Horizons, the story of the Rathbun Company and the Bay of Quinte Railway*. (Belleville, Ontario: Mika Publishing, 1983.) The "motors" appear in photographs at pp. 38 and 69.
12. Larmonth, op. cit.
13. *ibid.*
14. Carter-Edwards, Karen, *100 Years of Service*, [Cornwall Electric], 198-. p.56 ????
15. Linley, William R. "Canada's Last Common Carrier Electric Railway", *Newsletter*, June 1972. (Toronto: Upper Canada Railway Society).
16. *Poor's Manual of Railroads*, 1898, p.1129.
17. *ibid.*
18. DeRochie, op. cit.
19. Carter-Edwards, op. cit., p.58.
20. *Railway & Shipping World*, April 1898, p.52.
21. *ibid.*, August 1898, p.165.
22. Carter-Edwards, op. cit, p.65.
23. *ibid.*, p.68.
24. Incorporated in 1882 as Ontario Pacific Railway Co. Name changed in 1897 to Ottawa & New York Railway Co.
25. Carter-Edwards, op. cit, pp.72-73.
26. *Railway & Shipping World*, February 1899, p.59.
27. *ibid.*, March 1899.
28. *ibid.*, May 1899, p.218.
29. *ibid.*, March 1899.
30. *ibid.*, April 1899, p.119.
31. *Poor's Manual of Railroads*, 1906, p.1201.
32. Carter-Edwards, op. cit, p.91.
33. *Poor's Manual of Railroads*, 1901-1912 incl.
34. Larmonth, op. cit
35. *ibid.*
36. Carter-Edwards, op. cit, p.116.
37. Larmonth, op. cit.
38. *ibid.*
39. *ibid.*
40. *ibid.*
41. *ibid.*
42. *ibid.*
43. *ibid.*
44. Carter-Edwards, op. cit, p.116.
45. *ibid.*, p.126.
46. *ibid.*, p.167.
47. *Canadian Railway & Marine World*, February 1927, p.94.
48. Linley, op. cit.
49. *ibid.*
50. DeRochie, op. cit.
51. Carter-Edwards, op. cit, p.175.
52. *Canadian Transportation*, February 1943.
53. *ibid.*, September 1947.
54. DeRochie, op. cit.
55. Linley, op. cit.
56. DeRochie, op. cit.
57. *ibid.*
58. *ibid.*
59. Carter-Edwards, op. cit. p.185.
60. *Canadian Transportation*, August 1949, p.443
61. *ibid.*, April 1948, p.214.
62. *ibid.*, August 1949, p.443.
63. *ibid.*, September 1949, p.497.
64. *ibid.*, August 1949.
65. *ibid.*
66. Carter-Edwards, op. cit, pp.232-239.
67. Linley, op. cit.
68. Knowles, John D., personal communication.
69. Carter-Edwards, op. cit, p.249.
70. Linley, op. cit
71. Verbal communication from R.F. Corley.
72. Linley, op. cit.
73. Carter-Edwards, op. cit, pp.252-254.
74. Knowles, John D., personal communication.
75. Bytown Railway Society, *Trackside Guide*, 1989

Above: CSR 34 with a full load of passengers, possibly destined for a happy day at St. Lawrence Park. (Al Paterson collection)

Below: CSR 19 served Cornwall for twenty years after its purchase from New York, New York in 1928.

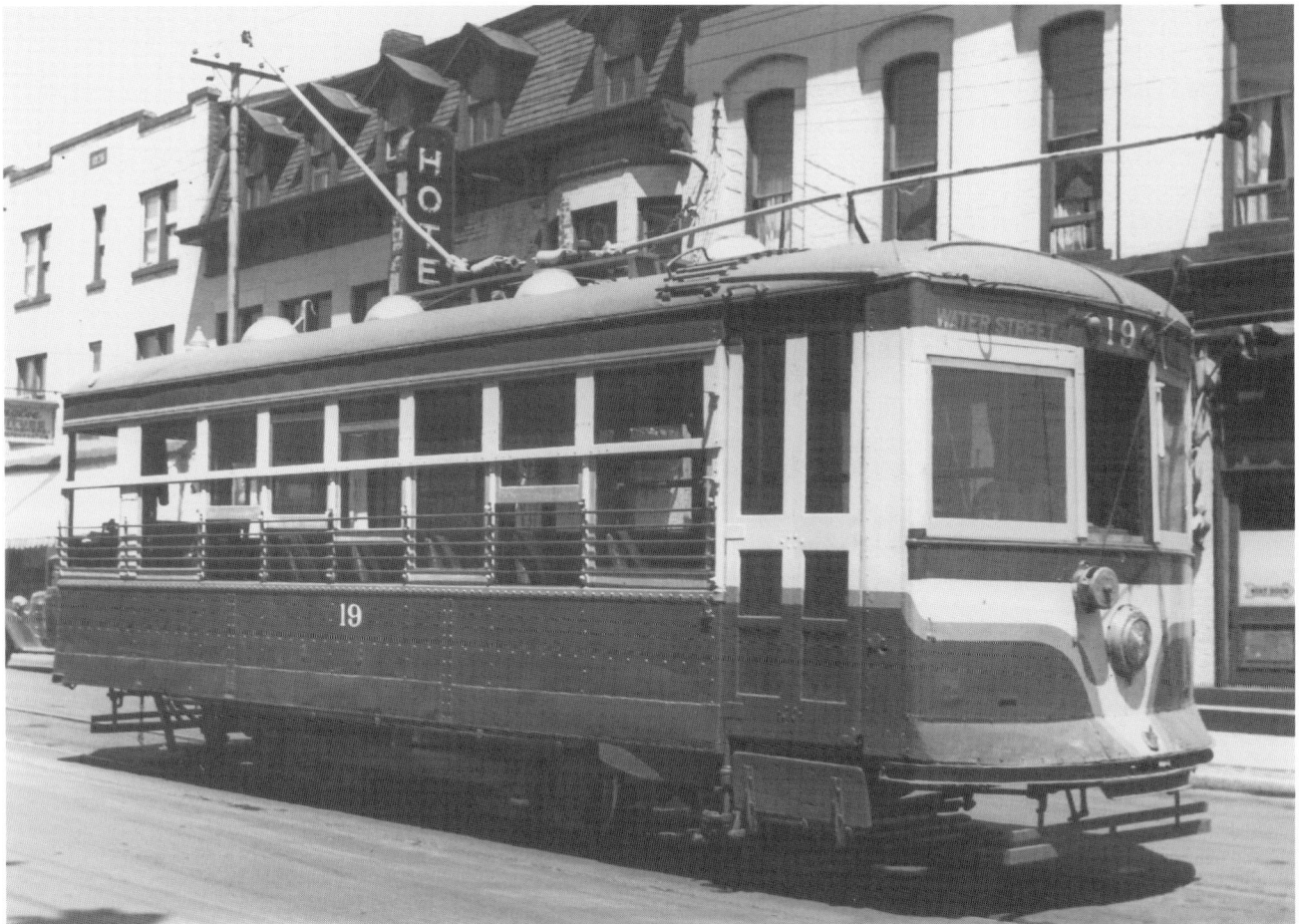

## SECTION FOURTEEN

# Authors, Maps and Photo Album

Anthony Clegg was born in Toronto, but moved at an early age to the Montreal area, and has lived with his wife Mae at their St. Hilaire, Quebec home for four decades. He began his career with Canadian National Railways in 1942.

Tony's early interest in railways was fostered by his aunt who took him to watch the trains from the bridge near Danforth Station, Toronto. As a teen-ager, some of his favourite birthday gifts were the railway passes to interesting places given to him by his mom and dad. Tony's father worked for Canadian National Railways until 1941, having been employed by its predecessors, starting with Canadian Northern Railway, in 1914.

An associate of the Canadian Railroad Historical Association, Tony was editor of Canadian Rail magazine for many years. He was one of the instigators of the Ferrovia railway exhibit at Montreal's renowned "Man and His World".

Tony's writings include Mount Royal Tunnel, and — with Raymond Corley — Canadian National Steam Power, as well as the recently published Self-Propelled Cars of the CNR. He collaborated with Omer Lavallée to write Catenary Through the Counties, as well as this book.

Omer Lavallée, a well-known writer, lecturer, editor, traveller, and museologist, was renowned as one of Canada's best-informed transportation historians. A native of Montreal, Mr Lavallée's career at the Canadian Pacific, which started in 1942, included a stint in the Paymaster's Department with trips to Maine to pay the employees in cash, before he was appointed to head the Corporate Archives section of the company. For a short time during this period, he was technical advisor to the director and camera crew involved in the filming of the CPR's film "The National Dream".

A predilection for the small, the compact and the quaint among railways and transit systems, and an insistence, at all times, upon factual accuracy in research, are traits which are readily apparent in the present book. His search for information about Canada's railways and streetcar systems took him and his cameras from Newfoundland to the Yukon.

Omer has authored numerous books and articles about Canadian streetcar systems and mainline railways, including Canadian Pacific Steam Locomotives and Van Horne's Road, the story of the building of the Canadian Pacific Railway.

His accomplishments as a foremost historian in the railway field led to his investiture as a Member of the Order of Canada, a distinction of which he was very proud to the end of his life in 1992.

*A number of interesting contributions have recently been received after the completion of the format of this publication. We think that what we have reproduced on the following pages will be of interest.*

**Below:** Base map of Cornwall from National Topographic series with the addition of CSR trackage in 1942, plus northeastern freight by-pass constructed 1945 - 1946. Does not show detailed trackage within industrial plants and yards. Map from Anthony Clegg walking over area in February and March 1942.

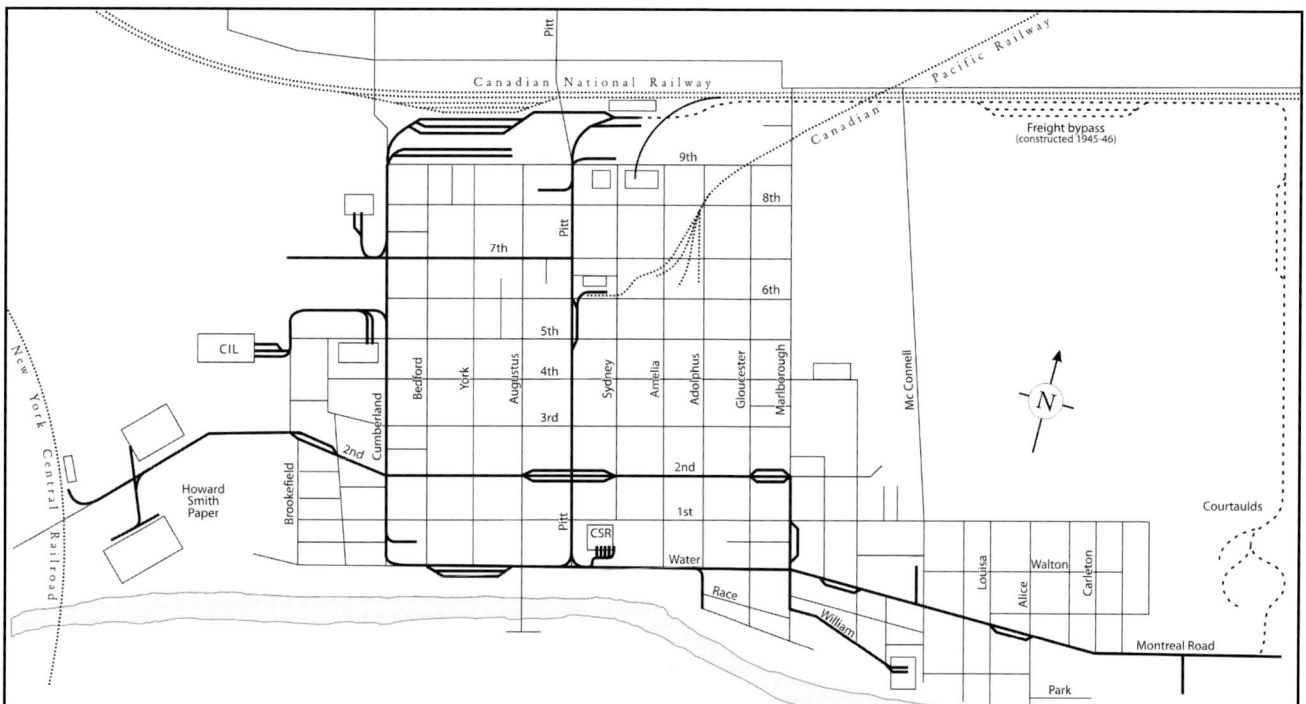

Top: Built by Brill in the 1920s as Toronto Civic Railway No. 67, later Toronto Transportation Commision No. 2230, then sold to Cornwall in 1927, CSR No. 18, a Birney Safety Car, is shown here on August 23rd 1943. (Brian P. Schuff collection)

Bottom: CSR locomotive No. 6 stands "at ease" outside the Water Street carbarn on July 5th 1948. A photograph of the same locomotive "in action" appears on page 72. (R.J. Sandusky collection)

Top: Cornwall No. 28 at CNR station as motor No. 10 switches the interchange yard on September 3rd 1946. (John D. Knowles)

Bottom: Cornwall No. 26 on August 23rd 1943. Received from Jamestown Street Railway. (No. 78). (Brian P. Schuff collection)

Above: This scene from May 1952 epitomizes the switching road. The moves are planned and CSR No. 8 is flanked by boxcars as it scoots up and down the interchange yard by the CNR station. Working the trolley pole keeps the brakeman on his toes (sometimes literally). (R.J. Sandusky)

Below: The motorman adjusts the trolley of CSR 33 in this wartime photograph. Compare with other views of the same car on pages 39 and 49. (Alan Maitland collection)

Opposite, above: Map of the trackage in Cornwall. This plan shows the trackage in 1966 after the passenger service on Pitt Street and Second Street had been abandoned. (UCRS *Bulletin*, 1966)

Opposite, below: CSR 33 providing transit service to the citizens of Cornwall during the 1940s. Compare with view of same car shown going the other direction on the opposite page. (Alan Maitland collection)

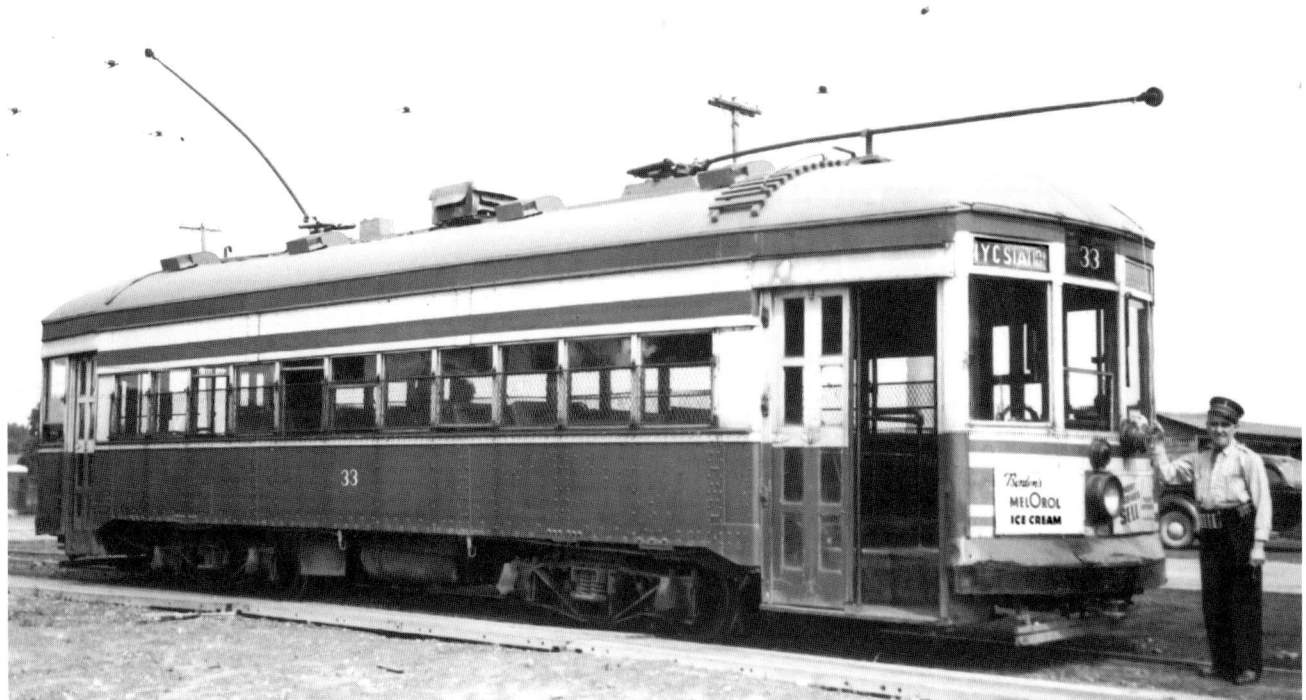

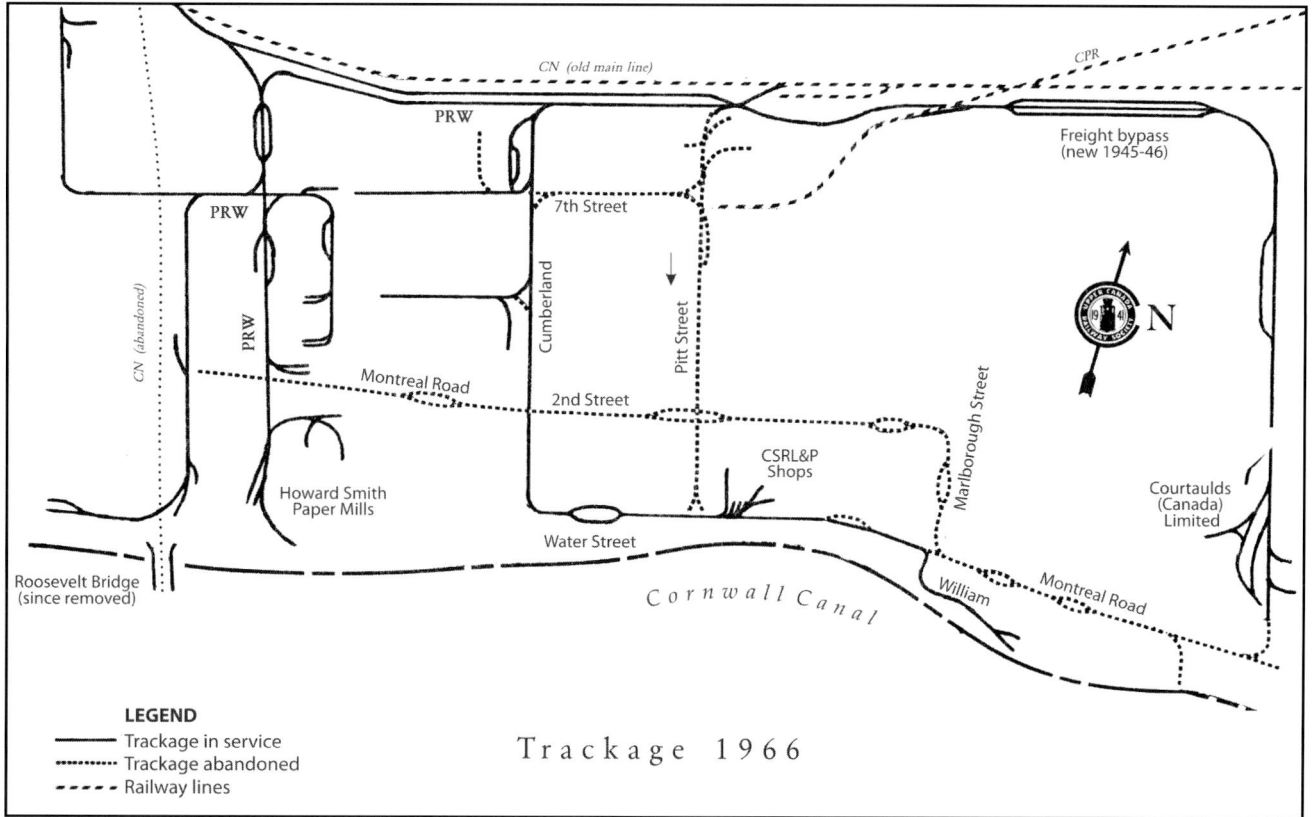

LEGEND
—— Trackage in service
········ Trackage abandoned
- - - - Railway lines

Trackage 1966

CN (old main line)

CPR

PRW

Freight bypass
(new 1945-46)

PRW

7th Street

PRW

Cumberland

Pitt Street

Marlborough Street

N

CN (abandoned)

Montreal Road

2nd Street

CSRL&P
Shops

Courtaulds
(Canada)
Limited

Howard Smith
Paper Mills

Water Street

Montreal Road

Roosevelt Bridge
(since removed)

Cornwall Canal

William

Opposite, top: CSR cars outside the Water Street shop on March 13th 1949 a few months before the final July passenger trip. Cornwall Street Railway No. 37 from Fort Wayne, Indiana; No. 25 from Haverhill, Massachussets; No. 26 from Jamestown, New York and No. 31 from Fort Worth, Texas. (John D. Knowles)

Opposite, middle: Late in the 1940s, many of the CSR's operating cars were kept in a yard behind the Water Street carbarn. (Omer Lavallée collection)

Opposite, bottom: Passenger service had been abandoned on the Cornwall system but work equipment was still required. In the car barn's

east yard on September 16th 1952 were CSR No. 31, used as a welding car, sweeper Fourth No. 1, previously Hull Electric No. 1, former Boston sweeper E10, and CERS Tram No. 29. (John D. Knowles)

Above: CSR Fourth No. 1, received from the Hull Electric Railway in 1947, clears the snow on the Howard Smith paper mill tracks as car 35 passes on Second Street on March 13th 1949. (John D. Knowles)

Below: Another wartime picture of CSR equipment shows locomotive No. 7 switching the interchange tracks near the CN station. Note the "V for Victory" sign in Morse code (...-) on the side of the locomotive cab. (Allan Toohey, CRHA collection)

# Half a century later...

THERE is not much in Cornwall today to remind one of the days when the trolley cars carried the citizens on their daily tasks – nor of the short-lived trolley-coaches that took their place. Both the Canadian Pacific and the New York Central stations have disappeared and the rail lines that they served have been abandoned. Canadian National and VIA are now located – well to the north of where the old Grand Trunk facilities were located. Even the former Cornwall Canal is now but a shadow of its former self, and the much larger Great Lakes vessels sail past the community on the USA side of the river via the St. Lawrence Seaway. The Cornwallis Hotel is no more and the once-thriving industrial establishment of Courtaulds (Canada) Limited has been razed. Reminders of the five cent fares that the people of Cornwall paid to ride their transit system have also disappeared, along with "the nickel ice-cream cones". Fares have increased along with the cost of the kiddies' treat and now hover between the dollar and the two dollar mark, while an unadorned postal facility has replaced the ornate structure shown in this May 1st 1949 photograph. (Anthony Clegg)

Opposite page, top: Riverdale trolleycoach, opposite the Cornwallis Hotel on Pitt Street, Cornwall. (John D. Knowles)

Opposite page, bottom: CSR locomotive No. 17, which had been on display in front of the Cornwall filtration plant since its restoration in 1981 under the direction of Donald R. Seymour, was moved to the Brookdale Shopping Mall at Brookdale and Ninth Street on May 17th 2005. In this photograph taken on May 30th 2005, the preserved locomotive is shown at the Brookdale Shopping Mall in Cornwall. (Robert Halfyard)

**About the Back Cover**

A CSR transit bus and an electric locomotive pause on Water Street, Cornwall, as the Great Lakes cargo ship *Bayfair*, from Brockville, Ontario, passes eastbound in the adjacent Cornwall Canal. (Ted Wickson)

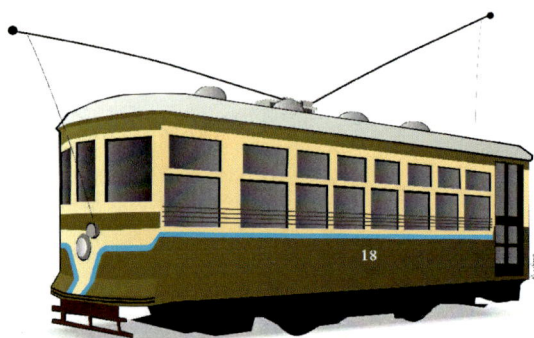

**Top:** Members of the Cornwall Electric Railway Society waiting to board CSR No. 28 for a sunny winter's day inspection trip over the system. The date was March 13th 1949.
(Allan Toohey)

**Left:** Prior to 1944 — when Cornwall Street Railway No. 31 was involved in a serious accident and fire, then later emerged from the company paint shop in red and cream livery — the colour scheme used for Cornwall's double-truck cars was a dark olive body with beige window frames and blue trim.
No colour pictures of this era are available since that was before the days of popular colour photography. The authors have therefore reproduced the colours as closely as they can be remembered, in the illustration to the left.
(Sketch by Eric Clegg)

**Bottom:** Still retaining its Ottawa Electric Railway number and livery, CSR sweeper B1 clears open track near the CN interchange. B1 and B2 had been built by the Ottawa Car Company for the Ottawa Electric Railway and both were sold to Cornwall after the abandonment of streetcars in Ottawa in 1959. They were retired in 1971 but Ted Wickson reports that the winter of 1970 was the "last hurrah" for B1 as the sweeper did not see action the following year. B1 was aquired by the National Museum of Science and Technology at Ottawa in 1971 and scrapped for parts. Identical sweeper B2 was sent to the Branford Electric Railway Society at Short Beach, Connecticut in 1972.
Photographed February 4th 1970 by W. R. Linley.
(Ted Wickson collection)

### About the Cover

Cornwall Street Railway car No. 29, newly painted but as yet unstriped and unlettered by volunteer members of the Cornwall Electric Railway Society, makes a photo stop during a fan trip in September 1950. The car is seen between the United Counties Historical Society Museum (left) and the Cornwall Street Railway's substation at the west end of Second Street. (Omer Lavallée)